Tracing the Rainbow

Tracing the Rainbow

Pablo Martinez and Ali Hull

British Library Cataloguing in Publication Data

A catalogue record for this book is available from
the British Library

ISBN 1-85078-487-6

Cover design by Diane Bainbridge
Print Management by Adare Carwin
Printed and Bound in Denmark by Nørhaven Paperback

Contents

Foreword

As a Pastor, I wish I'd had this book when I was starting out.
I'm very, very glad that I've got it now.

Ali Hull and Pablo Martinez have written with expertise,
grace and compassion about the most intensely painful and
bewildering time in life – the time of loss. Such a combination,
honed by study and practice, is of incalculable benefit when
we grieve; it's a lifeline when we are at the end of ourselves.
The factual information is clear and immensely helpful. Those
who grieve will know it to be a kindness to have it made so
accessible. The interviews are a privilege to read; direct
enough never to be sentimental and honest enough to be gen-
uinely useful. They are a profoundly moving testimony to
God's goodness. Read this if you need help in understanding
what's happening in your life. Read this if you want to help
someone who hurts because of loss. Read this to see that even,
in fact especially, in the bleakest passages of life, the colours of
God's love are traced upon our grey skies.

Then give it to your Pastor, who needed it years ago and
will probably need it this week.

Dominic Smart
Gilcomston South Church, Aberdeen

Commendations

Grief is the shadowy chasm that none of us wants to navigate, but it is the emotional geography to which all of us who love are ultimately called. This kindly, caring book will speak tenderly to those who feel bruised and lost by the devastation that grief brings: its grace-filled, crafted words will speak life to those who are wrestling with death. Thank you, Ali and Pablo, for your frank yet measured response to the subject that is usually greeted with uncomfortable silence.
Jeff Lucas, author, speaker, broadcaster

When you're bereaved, well-meaning people either avoid you or try to smother you. Here's a book that doesn't just give you clinical descriptions of what's happening (though it is full of useful information), but gets to the heart of what it feels like to be bereaved and how we can stay with people to be agents of comfort and support. There's also a gut-wrenching section on divorce as bereavement. No slick answers, but great material to help us mourn and grieve appropriately, held by the love of God.
Pete Broadbent, Bishop of Willesden

This book is warm, practical and honest. No-one goes through bereavement 'smoothly' and this book brings help both for those who are bereaved and those who seek to stand alongside

to give support. It will deepen understanding of death and our reactions to it, particularly when it is close to us.
Elaine Duncan, Scripture Union Scotland and Keswick Convention

This is a beautiful and loving book, gently written. In these pages are wisdom, guidance and pastoral comfort for the bereaved and those walking alongside them through their grief. Every pastor should have a copy.
Faith Forster, preacher, teacher and pastor, Ichthus Christian Fellowship

Woah, this isn't supposed to happen! I was skim reading *Tracing the Rainbow*, feeling nicely detached as I've never lost someone really close to me. But then, having come through a divorce and, more recently, terminal cancer (which has left me grieving for my previous level of physicality) I realised this book was actually very relevant to me. Probably to all of us, since we're all mourning something – if only that which has never been born. 'Blessed are those who mourn, for they will be comforted.' *Tracing the Rainbow* is a great combination of people's stories and experiences and expert analysis. This combination proves again C.S.Lewis' comment that reading shows we are not alone.
Rob Lacey, performance artist and author of The Street Bible

Death and bereavement are inevitable for us all. Yet often family, friends, and church leaders are fearful and feel inadequate. *Tracing the Rainbow* is a helpful resource for such times.
Ruth Calver, Ministry Associate, World Relief, USA

This is a much-needed book. How should we as Christians cope with bereavement, grief, loss, unanswered prayers and unfulfilled aspirations? The authors have sensitively researched this area of trauma, in the light of Scripture and case histories. An ideal gift for those in loss, wondering "why?"
Gerald Coates, Pioneer Team Leader, speaker, author, broadcaster

This should be on the bookshelf of every Minister, those who are committed to the pastoral care of those who are bereaved, grieving and mourning and will help many who have faced the 'long goodbye' of death. Written with obvious compassion, biblical clarity and from practical experience it is a real aid to improving and enhancing the practical pastoral care of the bereaved, whether by death or divorce.

The book is thoroughly biblical, eminently practical, well researched and the searingly honest testimonies from people confronted by the death of loved ones present an unavoidable challenge and an education for all pastors and grief counsellors.
Doug Barnett, preacher

I found this book incredibly honest, deeply moving and full of immensely practical and helpful advice.
Dianne Parsons, Care for the Family

A refreshing, honest approach to grieving which combines theory, theology, practical suggestions and story. This book will benefit anyone who has been affected by loss in any shape or form. Wonderful to read a Christian book which tackles the issue of the loss incurred through divorce. Every church should have a copy in their 'must read' library!
Jani Rubery, author, international management consultant and Spring Harvest speaker

When I have been with others who have been facing bereavement and divorce, I have felt helpless and limited in my ability to offer support. This book contains a useful combination of theory and case study and has given me greater understanding and confidence to face these issues in the future.
Jill Garrett, Director, Caret

This is a remarkable book; it provides a powerful combination of professional insights, biblical wisdom, personal experience and practical support. Profoundly human, helpful and hopeful.
Jonathan Lamb, Director, Langham Preaching, Langham Partnership International, Chairman, Word Alive

Many flounder in the face of bereavement, whether seeking to help or personally going through it. This book is an invaluable tool in understanding the complex process of grief. The inclusion of personal reflections and feelings are enlightening, the structure helpful and the tone objective but gentle. An invaluable aid for understanding the processes of grief, both for the bereaved and those seeking to help them.

Wendy Virgo, speaker and author

When our son died, my wife and I needed help. We were overcome with questions ranging from issues of Heaven to how to cope with grief. *Tracing the Rainbow* addresses many of these questions head on. It will be our book of choice to offer those who face the sadness of loss.

Lowell Sheppard, writer and Asia and Europe Director, HOPE International Development Agency

Trained as a medical doctor and psychiatrist, **Pablo Martinez** works at a Christian hospital in Barcelona. Besides this professional activity he has developed a wide ministry as a lecturer and counsellor. He has been a guest speaker in more than twenty countries in Europe. A member of the Executive Committee of the International Christian Medical and Dental Association (ICMDA) for many years, he is now one of its vice-presidents. He is currently president of the Spanish Evangelical Alliance and has been Professor of Pastoral Psychology at the Spanish Theological Seminary for seven years. He is the author of the book *Prayer life: how your personality affects the way you pray* (Spring Harvest Publishing Division and Authentic Lifetsyle) which is now published in eight languages.

Ali Hull is a freelance journalist and commissioning editor, working mainly for Spring Harvest Publishing, Keswick publishing and Authentic Media.

Introduction

A few years ago, a close friend of mine lost her baby son, who was stillborn. I knew that those who had been bereaved were often left alone and lonely: I knew I had to go and knock on her door; but everything in me screamed that there was nothing I could do, I would only make it worse, all she wanted was to have her baby back and I should leave her to her grief. But, of course, the choice is not between our hesitant words and regaining what has been lost – the choice is between those who know the mourner, doing their best to help and those, who know the mourner not doing their best. I did make myself knock on her door, I did sit and listen and cry with her, and our friendship went to a deeper level as a result. And I learnt that although we cannot turn the clock back for the bereaved, we can make sure that whatever they are going through, they don't go through it alone – unless they want to. Recently I have also learnt that people mourn very differently, and while one person will welcome the chance to weep with a friend, another will be struggling so much with their own emotions that they really can't cope with anyone else's.

So this book is there to help us understand what mourning is, and what we can do to help others or to help ourselves, if we are the ones who have been bereaved. There are many things that make it worse, and these tend to come up in the interviews – interviewees were asked: What did people do that made you feel worse? And: What did people do that made you feel better?

A huge thank you must go to all those who told me their stories and were brave enough to go into print, letting us use some of their most painful times to help others. Some of the interviewees wanted to remain anonymous, and we have respected this. To all of them, I wish to say an enormous thank you. All the interviews are either interspersed in the text or between the chapters.

Ali Hull

'Thank you. You were the person who helped me grieve properly; yes, you helped me cry after many months of silence, when I could not shed a single tear. Thank you very much; it did me a lot of good.' An old lady told me these simple words fifteen years after she had come to talk to me about the death of her son. I did not really remember the time when we talked, but her testimony of gratitude impressed me deeply and triggered a question which occupied my mind for a long time: what does it mean to grieve properly? In what practical ways can we help people during their bereavements? Are we prepared to help those who mourn? How should Christians grieve? Are death and bereavement different for non-Christians? If we were not created to die but to live, and death is something unnatural, then how does God view our mourning? Does faith in a personal God make any real difference in the grief process?

This book is the result of reflection on such questions. My work as a psychiatrist has allowed me to be in direct contact with many people afflicted by losses of various kinds. Here we will particularly deal with two losses: death and divorce. Our aim is to help those who have been struck by the pain of these two forms of separation. With this framework in mind we will consider grief from three perspectives: how it affects the mourner themselves; how the others around (relatives, friends, pastors) can help and how a personal God can change bereavement, opening a new window of hope. These three perspectives correlate with the three-fold purpose of the book.

- To help the bereaved understand better the nature of their pain and symptoms. 'Why do I feel or react this way?' 'How long will it take?' 'What's normal and what's wrong in the way I am thinking and feeling?' Having answers to these questions becomes part of the healing process.
- To provide practical tools to help those close to the mourner: relatives, friends, ministers. 'What should I say? When? How can I avoid saying or doing the wrong thing? What does the mourner need and how can I help?
- To comfort the mourner with the hope that the risen Christ brings as he emphatically said: 'I am the resurrection and the life. He who believes in me will live, even though he dies' (Jn. 11:25). A glimpse of the future life in heaven is the best antidote against the pain of the separation.

We tried to write a very practical book. People who are going through the dark tunnel of bereavement are not in the best condition to receive deep concepts or theoretical ideas. Understanding, comfort, sympathy, nearness and, above all, hope, are the main needs of the bereaved. Our goal is to help the readers to help themselves.

At the same time, it is my earnest desire to convey the deep richness that the Bible contains in this subject. I can witness from my own experience, both personal and professional, that there is a deep 'hidden room' in our heart that no psychiatric expertise or counselling can reach. It is a dimension related to our thirst for eternity because God has 'set eternity in the hearts of men' (Ecc. 3:11). This is why no writing on death or bereavement can be complete without the power of the word of God which is 'living and active' and ' more precious than gold … [and] sweeter than honey' (Ps. 19:10).

If we manage to help our readers to 'grieve properly' and provide them with light and hope in the obscure night of bereavement, this book will have attained its purpose.

Pablo Martinez

Understanding what is going on inside:

the steps of normal grief

Grief is the other side of love. It is the price in pain paid for the ending of a precious fulfilling relationship. In fact, it is an expression of love. Everyone who loves will experience this pain. The greater the love, the deeper the grief: as the proverb says, 'Real love will make you cry.' Grief is a universal experience, as old as the human race. Eventually each of us will die and in the meantime, all of us will grieve.

If we all agree that grief is a natural phenomenon after the loss of a loved one, then what is 'normal' grief? When does grief become 'not normal', even a disease? Where are the limits between both? This chapter will show in detail what happens when we lose a very dear person; our feelings, reactions, attitudes. This understanding is part of our own healing. The more we understand, the easier the recovery. Counsellors agree that if mourners can rationalise what they are going through, then they feel better. So this chapter is for those who are trying to help, and for the mourners themselves.

But we are also aware of a danger. Bereavement has been studied as never before. We have so much information today that we run the risk of overwhelming the reader. As J.I. Packer points out 'the elements in grief have been thoroughly mapped ... with a diligence that borders on the obsessional'.[1] Therefore, I will limit myself to those practical aspects that may become really healing to the reader.

Definitions

Two considerations are needed before we move on to the stages of uncomplicated grief. First, I will clarify the exact meaning of the three basic concepts in this book; bereavement, mourning and grief. Although they are not synonymous, these terms are often used interchangeably and I will do so as well.

Bereavement

This is the entire process of how one responds to the loss of a key person. One can also be bereaved of any important object: a possession, position, a pet, a part of the body etc. But these bereavements go beyond the scope of this book.

Mourning

This is the psychological process which accompanies loss. It also has a social dimension which helps to assimilate the loss: rituals which differ according to cultures. The funeral is part of the social mourning. Mourning covers the period from early bereavement till the mourner returns to normal life.

Grief

This includes all the subjective states that accompany mourning. Grief can be longer than mourning and may continue when the mourner returns to normal life.

---

[1] J.I. Packer, *A grief sanctified* (Leicester: Crossway Books, 1997), 164

Grief varies a lot from person to person and moment to moment. These differences are related to the mourner's personality, family background, religious beliefs and, above all, their relationship with the deceased. Because of this individualised pattern, any attempt to limit its boundaries is likely to fail. Each one of us copes with it in a unique way. Therefore, our analysis will be a description – how normal grief usually is – and not so much a prescription – how it should be.

Grief requires work

Secondly, some kind of effort is needed. Grief is not only something that 'happens to us', but something we do, and counsellors refer to this process as 'grief work' (a term first used by Freud). As an author puts it: 'It is work, hard, long, painful, slow, repetitive, a suffering through the same effort over and over ... breaking through the denial and disbelief that the past and the deceased are both dead ... until finally the past, like the lost one, is ready to be buried.'[2]

Grief is not just work, it is also a pathway. As you start, you hardly know how long it will take, or how dark it will be. You do not even know who, if anyone, will walk with you. Only two things are certain: there are no shortcuts and you will need to do the actual walking, step by step, actively.

> Grief is a journey – and it is a very long journey. People ask are you over it, like it is a bout of flu. You are never over it. You simply find a new normal – and it takes a long time. Grief is a journey of constructing a new life without the person you have lost and in the beginning you don't want that new life – you want the old one back.[3]

No one is carried through their grief, like a child, because bereavement is an experience that cannot be delegated and has no substitutes. Above all, you will not be alone as you

---

[2] Freese, A., *Help for your grief* (New York: Schocken Books, 1977), 48

[3] Barbie Reynolds, Interview, October 2003

walk along this pathway. The personal God who once promised Moses, 'My presence will go with you, and I will give you
rest' (Ex. 33:14) is the same who tells us through Christ: 'surely I will be with you always, to the very end of the age' (Mt.
28:20). The living Christ is with us and for us as we work
through our grief. The awareness of his presence is a powerful
tool to overcome bereavement.

> God was the one person I could run to – and I ran to him. He
> was my Rock and my Source.[4]

There are many similarities among the bereaved so we can
clearly identify the following common points. Any grief
process fulfils three great tasks or purposes:

- Untangling ourselves from the ties that bind us to the lost
  person; a deprivation experience.
- Readjusting to a new situation, new ways of living and even
  a new identity; an adaptation or adjustment experience.
- Recovering a sense of the meaning of life where the future
  looks attractive again; a restitution experience.

The mourner can usually accomplish these three tasks through
a period which has different phases. However, if grief is
delayed, absent or exaggerated, then doctors and counsellors
usually consider it abnormal, and we will consider abnormal
grief in the following chapter.

The stages of grief

Before we consider the stages of grief, let us look at one of the
most commonly asked questions: 'How long will it take?' There
is little agreement regarding the expected time which would be
considered as 'normal.' It greatly depends on the success of the
grief work. Nevertheless, one principle is universally accepted:

---

[4] Barbie Reynolds, Interview, October 2003

the length and severity of mourning are inversely related to the expectation of death. Widows who expect their husbands to die can cope much better during the first year than widows whose husbands die unexpectedly. The latter have far more distress and are more likely to go into complicated grief. This is why the so-called prevention of grief is considered so important and we will devote part of chapter 2 to preparation for bereavement.

Roughly speaking, however, most researchers consider a bereavement period lasting from one to two years as standard. Some years ago, the experts believed that one year was the average recovery time, but research today shows that this is not the case for many mourners. As a result, the time of bereavement considered 'normal' is now around three years. The exception is, of course, those deaths that are very traumatic, unexpected or where the person is very young. In these cases a period as long as four years is considered quite normal. The death of a child, however, may be so devastating that bereavement will last for many years, as we will consider in chapter 4.

Other factors also contribute to recovery. Most of them will be dealt with in chapter 3, on helping and counselling the bereaved. The duration of bereavement is less important than its direction, which is toward resolution.

Grief is basically a process of phases. Many experts on bereavement have proposed stages of normal grief. We have to bear in mind, however, that it is not a linear process, with precise limits, but rather a composite of phases which overlap and vary from person to person. It is perhaps more helpful to see each stage as a separate pool: with the mourner going from one pool to another in a random way, often visiting one pool more than once and in no set order. The process will be different for each person, and some people may miss out some stages altogether. What grief definitely will not be is a set journey, that visits set points, and lasts a predicatable amount of time. These stages should be understood only as guidelines, with indistinct transitions from one to another.

Grief is not linear ... grief is circular, and it is recurring. In one sense, you are going to live with that loss for the rest of your

life. The linear thing suggests you put the loss behind you and
you are completely over it and you don't mind at all. In fact,
your life expands and the loss becomes part of your life.[5]

Furthermore, the different symptoms that we will consider
usually occur in waves; they are not present all the time. This
means that they may come back when they are not expected,
when you believe that you are coping quite well. These fluc-
tuations are, therefore, normal and should not be understood
by the grieving person as a worsening or stagnation of the
process.

Most researchers point out four different stages:

- An initial period characterised by shock and denial
- A time of acute emotional discomfort with an intense
  search/desire for the deceased
- A later period of loneliness and social withdrawal
- Restitution

Let us consider each one of them in detail.

Emotional shock: numbness

This is the first reaction. It occurs immediately after the sad
news and may last from hours to weeks. There is a shutting
down of the rational and emotional reactions: 'I can't feel, I
can't think. I am emotionally paralysed.' It is expressed in
varying degrees of disbelief and denial: 'It isn't true; I can't
believe it.' Sometimes numbness is so intense that the person
seems to be in a dream.

> I just felt a deep, deep ache – it was like walking in a dream. I
> was dazed, on autopilot, with this deep ache in the pit of my
> stomach.[6]

---

[5] Barbie Reynolds, Interview, October 2003
[6] Peter Reynolds, Interview, 2003

This reaction is an unconscious, instinctive form of self-protection to diminish the trauma's impact. The mind and emotions become almost anaesthetised. The grieving person seems absent or indifferent, goes numb or feels dazed, as if unaffected. The intensity of this numbness is highest in the first three or four days. Sometimes the funeral service acts as an 'alarm clock', a critical point when the person awakens to reality. Everybody goes back home and you suddenly become aware of the unbearable emptiness.

> I was so numb, I found it very hard to pray, I couldn't find words. That is when I found written prayers, prayers written by other people, were the only way I could pray.[7]

The grieving person should understand that, because of this initial reaction of self-protection, there may not be much crying or pain at first. Some feel guilty about it: 'While I was at the funeral I didn't cry and I feel very bad about it. I don't think I loved my father enough', a girl told me, after her father died unexpectedly.

Does everybody experience this phase? No, numbness does not always happen; in fact some people think and feel surprisingly normal. When Job – a good example of normal grief – heard the news of the severe loss of all his children and possessions, he had an amazingly serene reaction. In full self-control, he pronounced these memorable words: 'Naked I came from my mother's womb, and naked I shall depart. The LORD gave and the LORD has taken away; may the name of the LORD be praised' (Job 1:21). Most people, however, experience some kind of initial shock when confronted by loss. The intensity of the numbness depends very much on the anticipation of the death: the more unexpected the loss, the greater the shock, and the harder it is to assimilate. This is especially true with the death of children or young people; even when the loss was anticipated, because we simply don't expect the young to die.

---

[7] Sarah Peacock, Interview, 2000

Paradoxically, sometimes there can be a sense of relief accompanying this emotional shock, especially when the deceased suffered a prolonged illness. The survivor often experiences the real numbness before the death on hearing the diagnosis or during the illness. There is such a lot of physical and emotional energy invested in taking care of the loved one, that death comes as a rest, for the deceased and the mourner. This relief lasts no more than a few days. Then all the anguish of the grief emerges. However, it is true that if death is expected then the mourning process starts before the death – it will be interrupted by this relief and then continue.

Acute mourning

> In the early days, I didn't eat, I just couldn't face eating. I didn't sleep well... I was functioning far below what I normally expect of myself but I didn't notice. I was far less innovative, far less aware of what was going on.[8]

This second phase begins when you are able to acknowledge the death. The survivor comes to a clear but feared conclusion: 'Yes, it happened, it's true. He isn't here any more.' Such an awareness will affect the emotions and the thoughts equally. Consequently, one of its main features is intense pangs of pain. These are 'exquisitely painful', as some describe them and occur in waves, and can last up to thirty minutes. They are characterised by uncontrollable crying, sighing, sharp emotional hurt; chest pain, feelings of tightness in the throat, shortness of breath, lack of muscular strength, light-headedness, etc. A woman who lost her husband described 'a wrenching of the gut.' A slight sense of unreality, fear of separation, restlessness and insomnia are other expressions of these feelings of distress.

---

[8] Sarah Peacock, Interview, 2000

> Grief to me is pain in my tummy. I just feel pain in the pit of my stomach. It was too deep for tears. I felt ill, I had chest pains.[9]

> We didn't want to be separated from anybody in the family, we wanted to be together all the time.[10]

These reactions are the result of a profound sense of loss. There is an increasing emotional awareness that the separation is irreparable. 'She won't come back.' So far this was just a thought; but now it has become a painful reality in the heart. It is not only the loss of the physical presence, but also the many associated losses: love, intimacy, security, identity, sharing, projects for the future and so many other facets that a rich relationship provides.

These pangs, therefore, are usually triggered by some reminder of the person's loss. 'I cry whenever I think of him.' 'I can't talk about my partner without tears in my eyes.' Such reminders are different for each person because thousands of memories come to mind in the first months. Actually the attention becomes selective, directed toward situations associated with the deceased. As time passes, these pangs dwindle both in frequency and intensity.

Bodily symptoms

The body is like a mirror that reflects the suffering of the mind. This is why during bereavement there are a lot of physical troubles: loss of appetite and weight, slow digestion, intestinal disturbances, exhaustion, lack of interest in sex, restlessness, insomnia, nightmares and dreams about the lost person are typical expressions of the deep distress. Sometimes mourners even experience changes in their body temperature which may rise as a result of stress. Loss of memory, inability to concentrate and headaches are also common.

---

[9] Barbie Reynolds, Interview, 2003
[10] Barbie Reynolds, Interview, 2003

Most often these body symptoms are transient, lasting only for a few days or weeks. But sometimes they have a permanent effect upon the health of the bereaved. In recent years attention has been focused on the increase in illness and a raised mortality rate among mourners, including those who divorce. The loss of a loved person is considered a precipitating factor in such diverse disease as asthma, tuberculosis, stomach ulcers, leukaemia and breast cancer. Even the grieving person's own death seems to be accelerated sometimes by a traumatic loss (accidents, violent deaths, suicide). The case is especially true with parents losing children. The reason lies in the powerful influence of the mind upon our immune system, the body's defences. The conclusion is obvious: bereavement acts as a powerful stressful factor which may seriously affect the health.

Yearning

Another feature of this stage is yearning. The survivor has an intense longing to reunite with the lost person. 'If I could spend one hour with him, I would pay all the money in the world', a widow told me, after her husband died suddenly from a heart attack. Such an attitude leads to a constant pining for the dead. A search for the deceased characterises a large part of this phase, especially in the beginning. As one widow commented, after her husband had been killed in a plane crash, 'I think I keep seeing him walking, when I'm in a mall.'[11] Many efforts are devoted to undoing the loss. All the mourner's psychological resources seem focused on achieving reunion. In fact, the memories of the deceased are at times so intense as to border on perceptions: 'I've seen her'; 'I heard his voice.' Some researchers even claim that hallucinations are a normal experience during bereavement. In one study,[12] 46.7 per cent of the widows had post-bereavement hallucinations. Included in this phenomenon is

---

[11] Quoted by Joe Stowell, *From base camp to summit* (Carlisle: Authentic Lifestyle, 2003)
[12] Rees, 1975

a sense of the presence of the dead person: 'I feel as if he were here.'

It is important to notice, however, that these usual hallucinations do not change the course of the bereavement. The person remains the same emotionally. This has remarkable apologetic implications for us, as Christians. Some critics claim that the appearances of Jesus after his death were no more than this type of 'normal hallucination'. This argument proves to be of no consistency as the result was exactly the opposite: unlike the hallucinations in normal bereavement, the grief process of the disciples was dramatically interrupted and changed their thoughts and emotions. They were totally new people and their mourning ended altogether. I do not know any similar case in the history of medicine or psychology.

Crying

This is the central and most natural activity in bereavement. It usually occurs from the beginning. Together with anorexia and insomnia, it makes up the familiar triad of early grief. Why do we cry? What is the psychological explanation behind it? When all our attempts to put grief into words ultimately seem inadequate to us, then we need tears. It is a simple way to express the pain of the separation and the desire to recover the deceased and meet again.

However, we need to clarify some common misunderstandings about crying: overt sobbing and weeping is not the only outlet to our feelings in bereavement. Some people, e.g. those who are very good at putting their feelings into words, will not need to weep as much as others. This kind of control comes naturally and it is not imposed either by oneself or others. As we said before, people grieve in different ways and not everyone expresses their pain through crying. The popular idea that 'he never really grieved because he hardly wept' is not correct. In the same way that we should not repress tears, we should not force them artificially either. The 'quality' or 'normality' of mourning should not be measured by the amount of tears. Nevertheless, to shed no tears at all is not a

natural reaction and probably means the mourner is hiding
some problem that will appear later on (as we will see when
we consider delayed grief).

> You can't force yourself to cry... we wanted to but you can't make
> yourself. You long to cry. Sometimes you feel like your tears are
> all that you've got left to hang onto, that that's the only part of the
> relationship with the child that you've lost that remains.[13]

Anger

This is also a common emotion after loss, although not for
every mourner. Again it is the result of the repeated frustra-
tion of their attempts to regain the lost one. The sense that the
experience is unfair or absurd leads to protest. This is actually
the most common outlet of anger: 'Why did this happen to
me?, 'Where is God?', 'Why didn't you...?' Such questions
express resentment and can be directed at anyone involved:
relatives, friends, doctors, God and even the deceased. This
sense of unfairness leads us to argue with those supposedly
responsible for the suffering.

As Christians, this is especially important in our relationship with the Lord. Job's attitude illustrates this. For a long
time he argued with everybody: his wife, friends and especially God: 'Job ... cursed the day of his birth. He said: "May
the day of my birth perish ... why was I not hidden in the
ground like a stillborn child, like an infant who never saw the
light of day? ... I will say to God: Do not condemn me, but tell
me what charges you have against me'(3:1-3,16; 10:2).

Anger and protest are normal developments of grief. They
express a desperate and unconscious effort to reinstate what is
lost. Their outlet is an essential part of the healing process.
Repressing such feelings may lead to complicated grief. We do
not find a single grief situation in the Bible where the Father or
Jesus rebuke the mourners over their protests, including their
anger or hostility. God understands us because he created our

---

[13] John Risbridger, Interview, 2000

emotions and minds. There is no one better to sympathise with our suffering.

Anger frequently comes out in ingratitude and reproaches. The first words that Martha said to Jesus when Lazarus died were a sharp reproach: 'If you had been here, my brother would have not died' (Jn.11:21). She was very disappointed at Jesus' delay. As Jesus did, it is better not to reply to such expressions of anger. You cannot take them literally and doing so may lead to unnecessary tensions. The mourner is not actually against you, but against the situation.

Bitterness

Anger can become a problem when it leads to bitterness. Job said: 'I loathe my very life; therefore I will give free rein to my complaint and speak out in the bitterness of my soul' (Job 10:1). Bitterness is one of the attitudes that may alter and delay the resolution of the grief process, eventually leading to pathological grief. The word of God, many centuries before psychology pointed out the emotional dangers of bitterness, already warned us about this attitude which can quench the Holy Spirit (Eph. 4:30,31) and become a sin.

The bitterness of bereavement is well illustrated by another Bible character, Naomi. She had gone through an extremely painful experience when she lost her husband and her two sons, in quite a short time. In the book of Ruth we find a woman torn into pieces. Her words reveal her acute pain: 'Don't call me Naomi ... Call me Mara (which means bitter), because the Almighty has made my life very bitter' (Ruth 1:20). Notice her anger and protest : 'It is more bitter for me than for you, because the LORD's hand has gone out against me' (v.13). She blamed God for her tragedy. Yet we could say that hers was a typical grief process.

Guilt

This is one of the most disturbing feelings in the whole process. The grieving person fears they may have contributed

to the death of the loved one, and this produces unbearable
pain. Whether by omission, 'something I should have done',
or commission 'something I did wrong', guilt feelings over-
whelm them. One of the most common regrets, with its
accompanying guilt, has to do with the deprivation of affection or support: 'I didn't tell him properly that I loved him'; 'I
didn't show her how much I loved her'; 'I should have been
more gentle'; 'I wish I'd expressed my feelings more openly.'
At other times, the regrets and guilt are about practical items
or decisions: not choosing the best doctor or hospital, being
too late for an early diagnosis, not pushing the person hard
enough to stay at home the night of the accident, not preventing them smoking and so on.

> I blamed myself. How much of this was my fault? I was con-
> scious that when I heard the news about the accident I wasn't
> praying. Why on earth wasn't I close enough to God to know
> my son was struggling for his life? The overwhelming sense
> was, if anyone was at fault, it was me.[14]

It is important to understand the psychological origin of such
guilt. Usually, this sense of responsibility for the death does
not correlate to any real objective mistake. Despite what the
mourner believes, it is not guilt that causes pain, but pain produces guilt. Guilt is the equivalent of crying, anger or bodily
symptoms: different ways to show the anguish inside.
Therefore the mourner should understand that their guilt is
false and will diminish as the grief comes to its resolution. This
awareness usually helps the bereaved. Often the expression of
guilt amounts to a search for reassurance that everything possible was done for the deceased.

Guilt becomes an outstanding feature of grief when the
death is the result of suicide. This is one of the most traumatic
losses and is likely to cause prolonged grief. The subject of suicide is so special and sensitive that it would require a whole
book to do justice to it. It is enough to say here that in most

---

[14] Peter Reynolds, Interview, October 2003

cases of suicide, there is a psychiatric disease behind it – major depression, schizophrenia or severe personality disorders are the most common ones. This does not relieve the pain of the parents, partners or relatives, but this fact has important implications for Christians. While it is true that lives belong to God and no one has therefore the right to take their own life (so suicide can never please him), on the other hand our Lord will undoubtedly take into account that the decision was not taken in full conscience, but under the effects of the disorder. This fact brings forth a ray of new hope to the relatives, who are left to live with the overwhelming despair.

Guilt can also be experienced in other less common forms. One is the so-called 'survivor's guilt': 'Why him and not me?' This happens especially to parents after the death of their children and in widowhood. This stage reaches a peak after the loss and then gradually decreases. We have to distrust quick recoveries. Unnatural relief may hide the repression of feelings and leads to pseudo-acceptance. Pain takes its time.

Loneliness and withdrawal

As tears dry up and the feelings of the acute mourning phase lessen, later symptoms of bereavement can be much more distressing than the earlier ones. The central feature of this third stage is loneliness, which becomes more severe after the first months and may continue well beyond the first year. What are the reasons for such feelings? The mourner gradually comes to terms with the reality of being alone: 'He's gone.' 'She won't come back.' This painful recognition is now complete: there are no protective mechanisms any more and the struggle to search and reunite with the lost one definitely stops. The grief work focuses on untangling feelings. The ties that bound the mourner to the deceased need to be broken. The awareness of this progressive detachment lies behind the symptoms of this phase.

This loneliness is experienced even when we are with people. Consequently, the mourner paradoxically often prefers to be alone: 'I don't feel like seeing anyone. I'm better at home, alone.' Relating to others becomes a burden:

> We went to church late and left early. We just couldn't face people.[15]

Isolation is associated with loneliness, and then social withdrawal. Silence and loneliness seem, to the mourner, more adequately to express the pain than words or tears. Another explanation for this withdrawal is the conviction that 'no one, however sympathetic, will be able to understand my feelings, so I grieve alone.' Pain becomes something private into which outsiders cannot enter. Other mourners justify their isolation by deceiving themselves: 'I'm fine, I don't need people', which perpetuates a cycle of estrangement: the more alone you are, the more lonely you will feel. But the reality is quite different: grieving alone becomes an unbearable agony. Such a problem is aggravated by an understandable fact: friends who only a few months ago said 'if there is anything I can do…', now return to their own lives, ignoring the mourner's problems.

This period of loneliness when acute mourning and community support have ceased, is one of the most painful times. It occurs typically four to ten months after the death and becomes particularly intense in widowhood. When the death of a spouse leaves the widow alone, the loneliness is both specific, for the lost spouse, but also general for the companionship lost: 'I miss him so much … but I also miss what he meant to my life.'

Other psychological features of this phase include:

Apathy and aimlessness

Indifference and lack of interest permeate most areas of life: 'nothing interests me.' There is little inclination to look towards the future: 'I can't see much purpose in living. Actually, I wouldn't

---

[15] Peter Reynolds, Interview, 2003

mind if I died tomorrow.' The most simple tasks of daily life are very difficult, especially getting started: the slightest effort can be too much for the mourner to make.

The mourner also seems dead to most stimuli. Their capacity for initiatives, for proper emotional responses, for empathy and even love dissolve. 'I can't respond emotionally.' When the English preacher Richard Baxter lost his wife Margaret, he wrote: 'I am under the power of melting grief.' Melting accurately describes this experience:

> For so many months, I wasn't able to think about anything other than the fact my dad had died. And there was that weight hanging over me the whole time, the feeling that something was not right.[16]

The symptoms at this stage resemble depression. Even some researchers refer to this phase as 'depression.' But the depression found among mourners differs from the spontaneous despair shown by psychiatric patients. We know that depression is a disease which requires specific diagnostic criteria, which include more than sorrow, crying or lack of energy. Normal grief is not depression. Clinical depression is only present in complicated grief. This is why the use of anti-depressant medication has very limited use here and in some cases may delay restoration. Medication should not be used routinely in normal bereavement because it blocks the normal 'maturation' of the process. Only some cases of pathological grief will require the use of anti-depressants or tranquillisers.

Anxiety and despair

Unlike the early stages of grief, the anxiety now is not caused so much by the separation from the loved one – separation anxiety – but by the uncertainty of the future. Lots of practical questions puzzle the mind of the bereaved:

---

[16] Sarah Peacock, Interview, 2000

'How will I survive without him?' These concerns emerge
from the insecurity of living without the support of the
person who was a source of reassurance, especially the
spouse. This fearfulness applies particularly to the present
family lifestyle in our Western society: high levels of indi-
vidualism and the loosening of the extended family ties
cause many widows to live alone with serious financial
problems.

This anxiety is aggravated by the bereaved's frequent
difficulty in thinking as clearly and quickly as before the
death. A certain degree of mental disorganisation affects
them: forgetfulness, distractibility, lack of mental clarity,
poor concentration, all these increase their sense of insecurity: 'I make a lot of mistakes; I find it more difficult to
take decisions, even small ones.' Consequently their
behaviour becomes disorganised too: 'I don't know what
to do, where to go, how to manage. I feel lost.' Although
these states occur most often in the first months of
bereavement, they may persist for a long time in varying
degrees of intensity.

Anniversary reactions

Most people who are grieving also experience these. The
first Christmas, birthday, wedding anniversary etc are
especially difficult dates because they bring back very
vivid memories to the mind. The emptiness and the separation are felt in a very intense way on these dates. This
kind of reaction is, of course, much stronger during the
first year, but it may continue for a long time. This is not a
symptom of abnormal grief unless it becomes crippling.
Usually the pain of the anniversary reactions gradually
dwindles. A memory is like a scar on your skin: you notice
it is there, but it is not aching any more. A memory, however, can also be like an open wound that, as soon as you
touch it, starts bleeding again. This is what happens, once
more, in the anniversary of the death of a child and in some
cases of divorce.

Identification

This is another feature of this intermediate period: trying to behave, dress, and live as the deceased would. It is an unconscious adoption of their personality. Identification seeks to perpetuate the memory of the loved one: 'He is not alive any more, but I like to do all the things he wanted,' said a young teenager who lost his brother in an accident. Associated with this attitude may be a desire to talk a lot about the deceased. The grieving person takes advantage of any opportunity to bring them into a conversation. Sometimes this causes tension among the rest of the grieving family, who may desire the exact opposite – not to talk about the lost person at all.

Sometimes the mourner's desire to be alone is so intense that it leads to a psychological problem called estrangement. This is a severe form of loneliness and inhibition, more likely to occur in cases of sudden death or losing children. It is like the end of life for the bereaved too. They unconsciously believe that 'going back to normal life would betray my love.' It is a symbolic way of dying together and thus identifying with the deceased. Of course, this has a big impact on the rest of the family, especially if there are other children whose care is, therefore, neglected.

Making wrong decisions

This is another danger at this stage: the bereaved may rush into a hasty marriage, sell all their possessions, including the house and move to an even stranger environment where everyone is new and so on. These are all unconscious ways of trying to kick-start a new life, of forgetting the pain more quickly, but such ways will probably result in greater problems and won't help the grief. Mourners should be very cautious in taking major decisions during the grief process. The mind is not ready to think clearly, so unwise decisions are likely.

The ability to tolerate this stage and to reorganise so as to direct the emotional energy toward new goals – adaptation – is necessary for the eventual resolution of grief. It is important to mention here that early childhood separations, how they were experienced and how they were dealt with by our parents, will greatly influence our future ability to cope with loss. The more difficult we find it to accept the loss, the more resistance to change and the longer the process will take. In normal grief, however, a final period of adaptation follows this hard time of loneliness and withdrawal. The end of the way seems near now.

Adaptation

Several words have been given to this final stage in the grief process: resolution, restitution, recovery and others. All these terms convey different valid goals: the restoration of energy, the readjustment to changes and others. It is a culminating period when there is a gradual return of a feeling of well-being, with the ability to adapt to daily life again. The hallmark of this stage is the ability of the bereaved to recognise what the loss meant to them and yet be able to return to work, experience pleasure and restart relationships.

How can we know that the mourner has reached this restitution stage? Are there any objective criteria? There are some guidelines which are the result of hundreds of studies; they will help us measure the recovery.

Recovery from grieving can be defined as a return to previous levels of functioning. As this is an abstract concept, we will use a listing of reasonable expectations, following the outline of an expert researcher on the subject (Robert S. Reiss). He mentions five capacities that we should expect from a mourner as a demonstration of recovery:

- Ability to give energy to everyday life
  'He died, yes; but I am alive and I have to live', were the words of a widow aged forty-five. Her sentence captures the situation of the bereaved at this stage: they are now able to invest their emotional energy in the present. In this way they are able to meet the challenges of everyday life. Up to

now, all their energy was devoted to resolving the grief process; all their efforts were bound and absorbed by the loss experience. Failure to recover will lead to them still seeing their current life as empty and meaningless.

- *Psychological well-being as demonstrated by freedom from pain and distress*

  Effective functioning requires that thoughts and feelings are not disturbing any more. Memories are not associated with unbearable pain, at least the pain does not paralyse the mourner's functioning. They can think and talk about the deceased without anguish. It is not unusual for the mourner to experience such memories at this stage as pleasant. When this happens, it means that a good degree of emotional acceptance has been achieved. Failure to recover is expressed here by an identification with the state of grieving to a point that freedom from it provokes anxiety: 'I feel I don't have the right to be well.' The bereaved clings to grief unconsciously as an expression of respect or love to the deceased.

- *Ability to anticipate and feel pleasure*

  The mourner is able to experience positive emotions such as joy, gladness and pleasure again. Failure to recover would be demonstrated by a state in which pleasurable situations are seen as meaningless. Some mourners even feel guilt or remorse: 'I can't enjoy it because someone is missing.'

- *Hopefulness regarding the future*

  The mourner recovers the sense of the future. So far they have lived either in the past – memories – or in the present – pain, anguish. All their thoughts and emotions were concentrated on yesterday or today. Now the future seems meaningful again. They want to plan activities, relationships etc. for tomorrow. Failure to recover is exhibited by the belief that the future is empty and hopeless.

The achievement of this stage requires a satisfactory degree of rational acceptance; not only a matter of feelings, but also of thoughts. A central ingredient in reaching such acceptance is the ability to develop a satisfactory explanation

of the causes of the loss: 'It was God's purpose for him. God
has the keys of life and death' etc. If the mourner cannot
reach a rational acceptance for their loss then they are more
likely to be troubled by guilt and this will make the grieving
process much longer. It is here where faith plays a key role in
this movement towards recovery, as most researchers,
including non-Christians, agree.

- *Ability to function socially*
  The mourner can once again relate adequately as spouse
  and parent, roles that are often seriously diminished by the
  grief process. This gradual return to recovery allows them
  to maintain emotionally significant relationships, that is
  loving, caring, self giving etc. The ability to start new relationships is also a good symptom of recovery. Failure in
  this area is shown by unpredictable behaviour, in both old
  and new relationships. The bereaved has strange reactions
  which are difficult for others to understand.

At least some degree of these five abilities is required to be
able to speak of resolution of the grief process. But some
realistic considerations are needed. Most if not all bereaved
individuals never totally resolve their grief. It is not like
influenza where you recover 100 per cent without any damage. We earlier considered the permanent effects that grief
may have upon health. Likewise, bereavement can bring forth
long-term consequences at a psychological level. After the
bereavement, the person is never the same as before. Grief, no
matter how well you emerge from it, produces some kind of
character change.

Should we conclude, then, that grief is a never-ending
zigzag process? Is it normal for the mourner to continue to suffer the same symptoms mentioned in the first stages? By no
means. If this is the case, then there would be no resolution,
but a complicated or pathological grief. But after a severe loss,
our identity will not be the same. A new image of ourselves is
developed. Our connection to the lost one is seen as part of the
past, rather than a present self. The more severe the loss – e.g.
parents losing a child – the greater this change in character

and identity. Some widows and widowers are very right in saying: 'You don't get over it. You get used to it.'

These changes should not be considered something negative. We need to remember a basic principle of grief. It can be an opportunity for personal growth. When mourning is over, a whole new person emerges. There are new attitudes, new values, a new vision on life itself, new relationships. With other kinds of suffering, mourning provides a genuine opportunity for change and growth. Any crisis brings forth dangers, but also opportunities; they come inseparably linked. For this reason, a proper management of this process is vital to avoid the pitfalls that lead to complicated grief.

This opportunity for growth is particularly true for Christians. James Packer, in his book *A grief sanctified*, refers to this idea of the sanctification of grief as one of our duties and privileges in bereavement. Packer reminds us of the Puritans who desired to sanctify every experience in life, including death. This meant having the right attitudes, reactions that may honour God, be a witness to others as far as possible and helps us grow as disciples of Jesus Christ.

We find a similar pattern in many other situations in life requiring acceptance. Any kind of suffering – such as loss – is not good in itself. We were not created to die, but to live; not to experience separation, but to be together. In this sense, death is not a natural phenomenon because it is far from the original plan of our Creator for us. Death is a 'normal' fact in as much as it is universal, but is unnatural and repulsive. For this reason we will never be able to accept fully what is against our nature as it was originally given by God to us. This is the ultimate reason why Christians grieve too. When a believer leaves this world, we are certain that he goes to a better one. But this hope will not automatically stop our crying because the pain of grief is the same. The future is certainly different, but the trauma of the separation now is the same as that of a non-Christian.

The Bible clearly states that death is an enemy; it is not presented as something acceptable or beautiful. This is why we find numerous examples of grief in the Bible, including Jesus himself grieving. Faith, however, changes the 'quality' of our

tears; it is a different kind of weeping. '... we do not want you
to ... grieve like the rest of men, who have no hope' says Paul
to his readers in Thessaloniki (1Thes. 4:13). As a believer you
cry, but you cry differently because death is not the end.

* * *

Sue and Alan Sutton lost their son Chris when he died of cancer. He
was a young man with everything to live for: he had a good job, he
was involved in a church and he was engaged to be married. The
interview took place less than a year after his death.

Sue Sutton

I think you get carried along with everything that is going on – even
the funeral wasn't as bleak as it could have been – it was a thanks-
giving service for his life, I didn't feel awful. It gets worse as time
goes on, you realise it really has finished and he is not going to come
back. It doesn't get easier, it gets harder. You cope ... you arrange a
few things, weekends, you work at living. Even now, we are moving
time along. We went to Bruges for a weekend break, and that was
quite good, but you come home and you think – nothing has
changed.

Every day when you wake up you have a mountain to climb. I
don't want to be melodramatic but at the same time you don't want
not to feel like that. I would hate to wake up and find that I didn't
miss him any more. Somebody said to me that there will be a day
when I can, and I shan't need to feel guilty about it, but I can't imagine that. Everything we do, I think he should have been here, or he
would have liked that; in everything he is our first point of reference.
He was very special.

He was very open, he would phone up and chat. I have no regrets
in my relationship with him. I am really pleased about that. I don't
know that I could have coped with saying goodbye ... I shared with
a lady at work whose son had cancer for three or four years – she
wasn't a Christian – and said to her our life on earth is just a tiny part
of eternity and shared all the things I thought as a Christian; two or
three months down the line I was going through the same thing and

you think – the words are so empty! It is so easy to say but the reality...

When we had Chris cremated – we never thought it important to tend a grave or anything like that, never thought whether it was right and wrong – and even that was hard, because I thought at one point, even his body has gone now. I know our bodies are not what is important but I miss it. I know I will see him again one day but it won't be like it is now, where he could walk into the room and I could give him a hug. I don't know what it will be like: I don't know what he is doing now or if he is doing anything – and I would like to. It doesn't help thinking about heaven. It would help enormously if I could think of him having a wonderful time worshipping God ... I don't know enough about heaven and I still feel that Chris is missing out. I know as a Christian I shouldn't feel like that, but he had so much going for him, he had bought his first home, he was so looking forward to being married, they are talked about exactly how they were going to decorate the house and Hannah has done it the way they were going to do it ... in the way they had planned – and in a way I feel that he was robbed. And I shouldn't feel like that ... and I know that getting out of the way I feel is all in my own hands.

Sundays are really tough still, it is a real effort to go to church, because of the things that we sing, and things that are said. I go through the motions and give it all to God, and say 'You are sovereign' but in my heart I find it really, really hard, and I suppose, in a sense, if I am really honest, I blame God because He didn't do what I wanted. I know God knows best. But so many people were praying so why didn't it happen? Why wasn't he healed? There was so much he still wanted to do...

The thing we found most difficult is that very few people want to talk to us about Chris. I will talk about Chris normally, and I think some people find that difficult, they think we should have moved on. I want to talk about him, he was with us for 25 years and it helps to talk about him ... People like Lynn Maskell will phone me up and talk about Chris all the time. I do find it helpful talking. I don't mention Chris in order to upset people, I just mention him because he is still part of our lives.

Physical effects – in the early days I used to go to bed very early. I didn't have depression, but I can understand people who do have depressive illnesses take themselves to bed, you don't have to face up to things ... I used to go to bed early but you don't necessarily go to sleep very early, you start thinking. I wake up in the night – I wouldn't wake Alan up, I am the sort of person who copes better grieving on my own – and if Alan was OK, I could cope. If he was down, that was difficult. It was easier coping on my own and crying on my own.

I must admit I don't pray as I used to pray because sometimes I feel I am being a bit of hypocrite. I am blaming God. I know he is sovereign, I know Chris is better where he is, but I still think he is missing out.

I haven't been angry, just very sad. Questioning – could we have done it differently, could we have done anything else ... As a mother you take your child's pain totally – obviously I went through that, I wished it had been me, but also I think – he had so much to live for, and it wouldn't have mattered if I had had ten children, it really wouldn't, Chris was Chris. It is not because he was my only son or because he was my baby, it was because he was him. You can't replace an individual.

When it first happened and we stepped back from church things, you find you are very lonely because you don't actually see anyone. Alan said 'please invite us round for coffee.' People did for a little while ... it is not just you miss the person but you have all the time you would have spent with that person so you have much more time on your hands. Suddenly you are trying to fill the time, you have too much time to think about things. We do have reliable friends, who have us round for meals ... whatever they do, the situation is the same. But they can help get through the time.

As a Christian, you think you should be victorious over all this, but it is hard, it is tough.

Alan Sutton

I felt a tremendous sense of loss, a mixture of loss, guilt – guilt because there is often a tendency with fathers to try to live their lives through their sons and I had to ask myself did I push Chris into things that he might not have gone into otherwise, did I have too high an expectation of him? – I am totally at peace about the way his life went, I believe that was all of God. I believe he had a very real calling on his life which we saw worked out; we would have liked to have seen it worked out even more, but that is the mystery, did he fulfil all that God had for him? I do believe that God is sovereign, and that he was sovereign in Chris' life and in Chris' death.

I don't have any guilt now, but the loss will never go away – my feelings now are of a constant loss, the memories are still painful but nothing like as painful as they were – the days of heavy blackness have gone, there were quite a lot of those, and a lot of crying, when I was on my own, I would just burst into tears, again that doesn't happen in quite the same way...

It certainly affected me spiritually. It didn't cause me to lose faith but it did make it very difficult – I couldn't pray, I couldn't read my Bible, I just couldn't do it. I had lots of questions and it was a physical act of will that got me into regular times with God and into my Bible again. It has given me greater understanding – I have always been a fairly compassionate person, I think – I am more of a pastor than a leader, because I have that sort of heart for people. You tend to attract the broken then. As far as understanding, I certainly have a better understanding of people's needs and the ways in which people deal with situations - and also my perspective on what is important and what is not has changed dramatically.

What did people do that didn't help?

People who have been through the same thing that Sue and I have been through don't automatically have the skills to counsel other people but they sometimes think they do. We have experienced that and it was very painful. We did have an experience of a couple who had lost two children – who came and spent time and did not know how to talk to us and it didn't help. It may well be that they were working out their own grief by talking to us, rather than helping us in ours. And the other thing I have found is that men are the worst at talking about their feelings. I have got very dear friends, men who I would lay down my life for and they have been there for me throughout this last year but the one thing that none of them has done is to talk about Chris – and that it what I want to do. I have to bring the subject up and even then they can't cope with it. I know it has been said so many times that the best way to deal with grief is to talk about it – and it is certainly true – but it is finding someone to talk to. It is very hard. There are others who have been very helpful … women are far more understanding and less concerned with becoming emotional, whereas for a man it is not regarded as the thing to do.

We went to see Peter and Barbie Reynolds some time last summer and I related so much to Pete – so many of the things that he experienced were identical to what I experienced. John and Lynn Maskell were at the end of the phone, they phoned every couple of days, right through the time Chris was in hospital; that helped. I have always been a naturally emotional person, and I am very touched by people's kindness so I was very moved by all the cards and flowers but the thing that helped me most was the letters of appreciation about Chris that we had. Sometimes from people we had never met … people Chris had worked with in the bank or wherever who talked about him in a really wonderful way and that helped tremendously because I think the biggest problem that we have had in coming to terms with the loss of a son at that age is what was their life all about? From the sort of letters we had it was obvious that Chris' life had been worthwhile even if it was a short one. Jesus didn't live much longer – so those were the things that helped. I said to Sue that we have never been ones for sending cards to people or letters of sympathy but I would certainly do that now because that was such a comfort. The memories are bittersweet – they make you cry but they also make you smile. Knowing that so many people cared about him and were impacted by him – that I found very helpful.

As far as work was concerned it didn't affect me too badly – I had very understanding clients, very understanding – who all immediately took my schedule away from me and said do it when you can, which was very helpful. I probably got lost in my work, I was able to. It wasn't easy, in fact it was very difficult, the fact that I worked on my own, there was nobody there to bounce off. If I felt down, I was down, and there was no one there to pick me up and you have to motivate yourself. On the other hand, if I was on my own and I burst into tears, there was no one there to be worried by it.

Sometimes something would trigger something off and I would think, 'Chris would like to know about this' and I'd want to email him. One day that is exactly what happened and it was then that the reality hit me. I couldn't do it any more. That was a hard day. It is like a dream, a lot of the time, almost as though it is a bad dream and you are going to wake up. I would phone him at least two or three times a week, we were very close, and you can't do that any more – there is still that feeling at the back of your mind that he might walk through the door at any moment and I wouldn't be a bit surprised. That never changes …

2

When recovery becomes difficult:

grief as a disease

'My husband died ten years ago, but my feelings are almost the same as the very first week. I still cry as much and feel such deep sorrow. I haven't overcome it. I can't get over the loss. Why? What is happening to me?'

These words show a universal reality: grieving is always difficult, but for some people it seems more difficult than for others. Why? So far we have considered the normal course of bereavement. We have agreed that, although grief is a very complex and varied phenomenon, we can identify certain basic features as the ingredients of normal bereavement. Sometimes, however, the mourner is unable to accept or learn to live with the loss with its accompanying feelings. It is too hard, too painful. Then grief is denied, delayed or prolonged. In such people the stages mentioned earlier are deeply altered. The process takes much longer than expected, or the feelings are not expressed in ways which relieve the sorrow and resolve the grief. In all these situations, we speak of pathological grief reactions.

Pathological grief
1 Identifying grief as a disease

'How do I know whether my grief is normal or not?' Most mourners, sooner or later, ask themselves this question. It is obviously important to realise when grief is becoming abnormal because then the way to face it changes totally. There are no adequate definitions amongst experts on what is normal or what is pathological grief. It could be defined by its intensity – this grief is excessive, or too superficial; or by its duration – she shouldn't have got over it yet, or he shouldn't still be grieving. But in the absence of a precise diagnosis of pathological grief, perhaps it is enough to use a subjective criterion; the mourner feels that they have not got over the loss – and should have done.

Pathological grief can be summarised in just one sentence: 'I feel that I can't live without them.' But, of course we need some objective indications to identify pathological grief. There are two features, found in most cases, which become the guidelines here. The bereaved will feel that

- The bondage to the deceased is so intense that they cannot free themselves from them
- They cannot cope adequately with life as a result of this abnormal bond. They cannot go back to normal life

These two common traits produce quite a number of things that deviate from normal grief. For practical purposes, we can classify them in three groups, which correlate with the three main psychiatric complications of grief

- Symptoms related to depression
- Symptoms related to behaviour disorders
- Symptoms related to anxiety

Each of these symptoms may also be present in normal grief, but they rarely interfere with daily life. When the grief is pathological they are more intense, last longer and become crippling. Both for the professional carers and for the mourner's relatives it is most important to identify when such disorders are happening. This is because these disorders can be treated, either with medical or psychological means, and the mourner can recover.

Depression

Depression and grief are closely associated in the minds of many people but they are not the same thing. Until recently, even the experts equated bereavement to reactive depression because some form of depressive reaction is very common after a loss. Some authors' research shows that almost 50 per cent of mourners had symptoms that met the diagnostic criteria for depression one month after the loss and 16 per cent at one year. This research shows us how closely related they are. Today it is agreed that depression and grief are different, though they may occur together and their symptoms overlap. For example, insomnia, weight loss and poor appetite, sad feelings and the loss of interest in life are present both in clinical depression and in reactions to bereavement.

If they are not the same, how can we differentiate adequately between both? The distinguishing feature between them is not so much the symptoms, which frequently overlap, but in their duration: they should diminish over time. This timing criterion is very important: if the depression persists, it means that the grief remains unresolved. So, clinical depression is an expression of pathological grief when it lasts more than twelve to eighteen months after the loss.

Depression in the bereaved can be identified by some of the following features:

- Increasing feelings and thoughts of unworthiness: 'I'm no longer valuable as a person.' Helplessness and hopelessness: 'I want to give up.'
- Subtle or declared ideas of self-destruction: 'Life is not worth living; I would rather be dead. I want to die.'
- Guilt feelings which can be obsessive and torturing: 'If only I'd been there when they died'; 'If I'd done so and so.' The bereaved feels intensely responsible for the death. Strong self-condemnation is the outcome of such intense guilt.
- Excessive hostility to a point to provoke tension in relationships. If it grows, it may lead to aggressiveness and behaviour disorders (not unusual in male teenagers).

- Complete and persistent social withdrawal including refusal to receive help or counselling.
- Extreme emotional expression such as constant crying.

Sometimes there is a sense of guilt at having participated in the event which caused the death. This is common with car drivers who have been involved in a crash in which someone else was killed. The survivor is very likely to have a difficult grief, which may become chronic. Paul Tournier, the Swiss doctor and author, in his book *Creative Suffering*[17] refers to when he had an accident in the car he was driving and his uncle died. Tournier was an orphan and this uncle had been like a father to him. The resulting guilt, to a certain degree, accompanied him all his life. In a small percentage of mourners the depression may be so severe that they are likely to commit suicide. Careful medical supervision and adequate treatment are required urgently in these cases.

Behaviour disorders

These can be expressed in different ways. The most harmless is hyperactivity. The grieving person chooses to be permanently over-busy as a way of forgetting or neglecting the pain: 'When I'm doing other things, I don't think of them. As soon as I stop, all the memories come to my mind.'

Disorders of impulse control. In some cases, a mourner's self-control will fail and they cannot control their impulses. They can't stop a drive to do something that will harm either themselves or others. Gambling, kleptomania and outbursts of hysteria are common impulse disorders. They discharge the tension accumulated inside. Impulsivity together with *irritability* form an explosive mixture which may seriously damage the grieving person's relationships with others.

Associated with disorders of impulse control are *excessive drinking and drug abuse*. Bereavement sometimes triggers substance abuse, especially of alcohol, but also of

---

[17] Paul Tournier, *Creative Suffering* (London: SCM Press Ltd., 1982)

hypnotics and tranquillisers. This can be an attempt to relieve the pain and the loneliness. 'I never had any problem with drinking before; but since she died, drink is the only way to drown my sorrow.' This pattern is not unusual in women going through a difficult grief, especially when they feel lonely.

In the worst cases, there can be *antisocial behaviour*. This is more likely to happen with teenagers in situations of risk; difficult family environments, being withdrawn, being unable to make and keep friends. Adolescence is a critical cross-roads, where taking the wrong way can have long-lasting consequences. This is why a grieving teenager should always be cared for attentively and given a proper follow-up. They are extremely vulnerable to the trauma of death, especially when a sibling dies.

Anxiety disorders

We have already referred to the high occurrence of separation anxiety in normal grief. The bereaved person often feels tense, nervous and fidgety, with a strong longing for the lost one. But besides this normal anxiety, there can be anxiety disorders which should be considered and treated properly by a professional.

As with depression, almost half of mourners experience some kind of anxiety disorder during the first year, particularly generalised anxiety and panic attacks. The person may experience breathlessness, a sense of needing air, sometimes severe enough to make them loosen their clothes or run to an open window. Dizziness and light-headedness are also common. The anxious person is dominated by a feeling of constant apprehension and fearfulness, with the idea, sometimes obsessive, that something bad will happen soon; an accident, a disease. They are dominated by irrational fears, including phobias. Eating disorders, such as bulimia or compulsive eating, are quite normal. They are an expression of anxiety and the problems with impulse control.

Special attention should be given to *post-traumatic stress disorder* (PTSD), a form of anxiety particularly associated with unnatural deaths. Some severely traumatic losses such as suicide, murder, accidents and collective deaths (e.g. plane or train crashes) provoke reactions in the bereaved that are different from normal grief. The survivors from natural disasters (earthquakes, fire, floods) can also often suffer from this syndrome. They can experience intrusive, vivid images of the death which are repetitive and disturbing. It is like re-living the traumatic event: 'It runs like a film in my mind, shown against my will and I can't turn it off.' They may also suffer nightmares, hyper-vigilance – being super-alert – with resulting fatigue and difficulties in thinking clearly.

Sometimes PTSD leads to the sufferer avoiding certain things: the mourner persistently refuses to go to places or use vehicles or relate to people that remind them of the traumatic event. The most characteristic trait of this disorder, the intrusive memories that reflect the scene of the death, require some form of professional treatment, either medical or psychological.

2 Types of abnormal grief

In the same way that normal grief varies from person to person, not everybody shows pathological grief in just one pattern. The experts have identified quite a number of subtypes of complicated reactions in bereavement and we will summarise them in three categories:

- Delayed grief
- Absent or inhibited grief
- Chronic grief

In each one of them we shall consider three questions:

- What are their defining features?
- When are they most likely to happen?

- How can we prevent these reactions?

Delayed grief

In this case the symptoms do not differ from those of normal grief. There is a proper expression of feelings, yearning, crying, anger etc. The only difference lies in its time of onset: grief is considered delayed when it takes longer than two weeks after the death to appear. Sometimes it may take months or even years. Eventually the grief starts unexpectedly, usually without any apparent reason or triggered by another minor loss which is much less meaningful. Likewise, there may be an exaggerated emotional response.

What is the psychological explanation behind this delay? The reason why the feelings are initially inhibited is that the pain is not intense enough to provoke an emotional reaction. It is like trying to start a fire when the wood is wet. Then another question comes to our mind: why is the pain not appropriate or proportional to the loss? Why does the grief get stuck?

One real example will help us understand the psychological problems in delayed grief. I remember a patient who, during a regular therapy session, almost by chance, told me that her father had died that very week. Surprisingly, she said it without any emotion at all, just as a simple piece of information. Such a cold reaction was totally inadequate for the death of a father. But three months later she came and burst into tears; she was deeply affected, had lost weight, could not eat and had many other typical grief symptoms. What had happened? Her cat had died a few days earlier. 'I can't understand it,' she said, puzzled. 'When my father died, I didn't cry a single tear; now that I have just lost my cat, I can't stop crying.'

Her family background helps us understand the story. The father of this young lady was an alcoholic, who behaved violently. She could not love him; actually she hated him. The father-daughter relationship contained no caring, no empathy, no exchange of the deep feelings involved in any love relationship. She was, thus, unable to build up any emotional investment[18] in her father, and therefore her pain was not intense enough to provoke the emotional response of grief.

This case reflects an important principle in grief. The pain caused by a loss is proportional to the emotional closeness to the lost one. Such closeness is established and enriched by the love – self-giving – we invest in the other person. Deeply relating to another human being implies some degree of mutual sharing of selves. It is like extending ourselves through another person. A part of my soul, of my heart and identity is linked to the other one. No wonder, then, that we suffer a sense of great loss when they die because it is like losing a part of ourselves. We have lost that part of ourselves we have invested in the other person.

The relationship between David and Jonathan in the Old Testament is a remarkable example of what we are saying. Their friendship was so deep that Jonathan's soul was 'knit to the soul of David' and he loved him as himself (1 Sam.18:1).[19] It is not surprising that when Jonathan died, David wrote the famous lament for his friend and, deeply moved, cried: 'I grieve for you, Jonathan my brother; you were very dear to me. Your love for me was wonderful, more wonderful than that of women' (2 Sam.1:26). The soul of David was lacking the precious part that corresponded to the love of Jonathan. This closeness is something different from dependency, as we will see later, because it stems from love. Neurotic or excessive dependency, on the other hand, is born from need and, therefore, is more selfish.

Absent grief

We could define this as a stoic refusal to show emotion or be affected by the loss. It is also called inhibited grief because they are both on a continuum. This inhibition is not always complete, there can also be partial responses with limited

---

[18] A term used in psychoanalysis meaning basically self-giving in a love relationship, e.g. parents and children.

[19] Translation from the Revised Standard Version.

expression of grief. Its hallmark is the absence of the typical expressions of bereavement described in the previous chapter, in such a way that the bereaved continue their lives as if nothing had happened. It is like a prolongation of the initial stage of numbness or shock.

There are two possible psychological mechanisms that explain this process. One is denial. The mourner unconsciously represses any emotion in such a way that an observer can't see any external signs of pain or grief. They are unable to express the impact of the loss; they do not feel the need to cry or show sorrow. The other mechanism is a conscious one, avoidance. They do not allow their emotions to come to the surface and usually they refuse to talk about the death itself or the deceased. A tense silence occurs when someone mentions anything related to the death. It is a conscious voluntary repression. In both cases any expression of emotions is too painful, so they deny or avoid them. This way, without realising it, the death of their loved one becomes like a collection of emotional 'pus' that can eventually cause some sort of psychiatric disorder.

> I refused to grieve. There was no one there to comfort me in my family and I was afraid that if I started to cry, I wouldn't be able to stop and might even lose my mind. So I bottled it all up.[20]

In fact, if inhibited grief persists, it may lead to major depression. The outlet of emotions is crucially important. We have this saying in psychiatry: 'an impression, without its expression, leads to depression.' For this reason, the use of medicines – especially anxiolytics[21]– may be very helpful in some cases to allow the emotions to come to the surface. As the anxiety diminishes through the action of the drug, the expression of feelings is less painful and, thus, greatly facilitated. It is like a key opening a door. We are not in favour of

---

[20] Annie, Interview, 2003
[21] Popularly called tranquillisers, they are drugs used in anxiety states. The most common are the benzodiacepines.

routinely using this kind of medicine in normal grief, but here it is a matter of preventing major problems.

> I hit a depression some months later, but still refused to go for any kind of help. I was a student at the time and the stock treatment for depressed students seemed to be Valium handed out by the sackload. I battled on through a series of other major changes and eventually suffered from all sorts of strange mental symptoms, including being able to hear burglars breaking into the house, day or night, when there was nobody there. [22]

In daily life, a signal of inhibited grief is the refusal to change the deceased's room, or to dispose of their clothing and other possessions. The grieving person shows a veneration of objects that remind them of the deceased in such a way that these objects become a kind of permanent link with the lost one. In normal grief it may take some weeks or months to do so, but a moment comes when the grieving person spontaneously feels the need to make changes. One word of caution here: it is a mistake, commonly made by relatives, to force a premature disposal of these personal belongings. I remember the case of a young widow whose sisters-in-law disposed of their brother's clothing and changed all the furniture in the room one day after the funeral. Even worse, they did so without the widow's participation. This is very harmful and causes a lot of resentment.

What factors contribute to this problem? The causes that we will mention are common both for delayed and inhibited grief. This is why we will consider them together. At the same time, our capacity to correct such factors will become the best way to prevent both kinds of abnormal grief. First of all, *past emotional deprivation*. Here the problem lies within the person. The grief process is altered because of traits deeply ingrained in the personality. These people are prone to repress the expression of any emotion, not only in times of distress but also in positive situations like loving relationships (marriage, friendships).

---

[22] Annie, Interview, October 2003

Their problem is due, most of the time, to the fact that they did not learn how to express affection when young. If children do not experience the warmth, care and tenderness of a loving relationship, they will tend, as adults, to repress any expression of emotions, being considered as cold, distant people. It is simply that they can't give what they haven't received. From their early childhood they found it difficult to speak a language they were not taught – the language of feelings. Of course, the more severe the deprivation, the greater their difficulty. We see, therefore, how our upbringing may influence the way we react to losses and grief.

Secondly, *current stress situations*. Sometimes the death of a loved one comes together with other life troubles: marital or family problems, sickness, financial difficulties, unemployment, migration, moving houses, etc. Special mention should be given to the presence of small children who need to be brought up by the survivor in the midst of financial pressures. During these times of stress, the grieving person unconsciously represses or delays the pain as a form of self-protection. They need their mental energy to resolve this current crisis: 'I have enough with one big problem, I can't take more than one at a time' could be the summary of this unconscious reaction. This way, the grief work is either inhibited or greatly diminished.

Along this line, the repression of grief may happen when there is a psychiatric disorder prior to the death of a loved one. This is especially true with major depression. One of the frequent symptoms of depression is the difficulty both in feeling and expressing feelings. A sense of having 'sleeping emotions' is very common in depression. Unable to love or feel loved, unable to enjoy any activity, even unable to cry, the person feels 'as though there is a high wall blocking my heart and stopping my emotions getting out.' In such a condition, the normal expression of bereavement is obviously altered.

Thirdly, absent or inhibited grief is greatly influenced by external factors. *Social or cultural* restraints can be a powerful repressing force in bereavement. In countries which value efficiency, rationalism and pragmatism, death can be seen as an embarrassment. It is considered a useless nuisance, as are all the other dimensions of suffering. This is one of the most visible features of a sick society, influenced by a pleasure-seeking culture which can't endure any form of pain. Grief is seen as inevitable, but it should end as soon as possible and emotional expressions are discouraged. It is noticeable how many medical doctors are embarrassed in the face of death. They are (in theory) the experts in human suffering, yet they refuse to get involved in situations where they have to tell patients or relatives the bad news of death. I believe this is symptomatic of the current social intolerance of pain and suffering. We prepare ourselves so much to live that we are not ready to die. It is here, therefore, that we can do some work in preventing inhibited grief through proper information and basic training.

Special attention should be given to the idea that, when a believer has died, fellow Christians, even those closest to them, shouldn't cry because the person who has died has gone to be with the Lord. This advice comes from a total misunderstanding of the nature of death and the pain it causes. Death is a devastating event because it is so unnatural: death did not exist in the original state of things – the Garden of Eden – and it came as the supreme enemy to humankind. When Jesus lost his good friend Lazarus and saw Mary and the Jews who had come along with her, weeping, he also wept. The writer summarises in a most simple sentence – 'Jesus wept'– the deep reality behind bereavement: death is always a painful separation. John used strong words to describe Jesus' emotions over Lazarus' death: 'he was deeply moved in spirit and troubled' (Jn. 11:32). The two verbs used here have a similar meaning to the effects of an earthquake and could be translated, 'his heart was strongly shaken.' If Jesus experienced such distress in the face of death, we can't pretend to be more spiritual than him by repressing our feelings. True spirituality never makes us less human. When Jesus wept, he was fully human and fully divine.

Chronic grief

Some authors call this unresolved grief because it may last for many years, sometimes for life. The process here remains unchanging; the symptoms are always the same, with no progress whatsoever in the various stages of grief. The person surrenders to grief, they never finish the grieving process. Several years after the loss, they behave as if the death were recent: crying and acute mourning symptoms are common. The mourner seems blocked, unable to walk any further. Bereavement becomes thus an unending pathway. A monotonous repetition of some symptoms, especially guilt and self-reproach, can finally cause depression, which is usually an associated problem these mourners. Other frequent symptoms are permanent withdrawal – a mourner who is suffering from chronic grief will stop relationships and prefers to live in solitude; or marked sadness, leading usually to bitterness and a loss of the sense of life. These are the main features of this process.

Who is more likely to suffer from this type of unresolved grief? Past losses and deprivations play an important role here, as we also noticed with inhibited grief. People who react severely to a loss and are unable to do the necessary grief work are often handicapped by earlier meaningful losses. The way a person has reacted to separations in the past is a good predictor of future reactions. If such losses were handled with difficulty and caused problems, grieving is likely to be complicated.

Once more, this is especially applicable to children who have lost a father or mother. Such an early experience makes them more vulnerable to the pain of further bereavements. It is like reopening a very painful wound which was hardly healed. They are not prepared to tolerate the distress of an experience which reminds them so much of the early trauma. Simply put, they lack the necessary emotional strength to face this 'echo' of the original traumatic event. A similar situation occurs with emotional deprivation. In this case it is not a literal loss, but the absence – emotional or real – of a loving figure that causes the increased vulnerability, as we explained earlier. . The lack of affection stopped the child from developing a healthy identity, so they are not ready to face separation in a mature way.

Chronic grief is also common in parents who have lost a child, frequently teenagers who died suddenly in accidents. According to researchers, mothers are more prone to this kind of grief. Their subjective distress can be so high that quite a number of them have serious health problems, even leading sometimes to premature death (e.g. of cancer). Chronic grief has a high cost also on the other family members, especially the children, as the father or mother do not function adequately in their relationships. The whole family life is thus seriously affected, with long-lasting consequences for the children's upbringing. Often the mother is unable to show any affection to her remaining children because she feels herself blocked. Her life has become a memorial to the dead child and she is unable to give herself to the other children. This situation can lead to the sort of deprivation that may eventually result in a depressive personality in the children.

It is necessary here to consider some unconscious reasons for chronic grief. In all these cases, there is a hidden motivation for the mourner to continue grieving. Some people use it as a way of denying the death of the loved one. They view the end of grief and going back to normal life as something offensive to the honour and memory of the lost one. Chronic grief is an unconscious attempt to keep them alive by making them into living memorials. This idea could be summarised in these sentences: 'I haven't got the right to feel well; if I don't grieve, it means that I didn't love them enough.' This way, grief becomes a distorted way of perpetuating the love for the deceased.

Others find in chronic mourning a way to cover up intense guilt. Sometimes this guilt is connected to unconscious hostile feelings for the person who died. Chronic guilt is almost always associated with a history of unresolved conflicts and emotional problems between the deceased and the mourner. Finally, others use grief as a self-imposed form of martyrdom through which they unconsciously get some psychological gain, for example attention or affection.

From all these considerations, it is not difficult to deduce that chronic grief is often resistant to treatment. It actually becomes like an unconscious umbrella, a protection from the real psychological problems that lie behind it. The grieving person does not want to relinquish their bonds with the deceased. Since this untangling from the ties that bind us to the lost one is the very essence of normal grief, then the whole process stops. This reluctance to accept the reality – 'we can't meet again'– is often related to the nature of the relationship between the bereaved and the deceased. It may well have been a dependent and clinging relationship. This will lead us to consider this relational factor in more depth.

One word of caution should be said here about the dangers of those around the mourner labelling their grief as 'chronic', simply because they would like the bereaved to move on more quickly. Sometimes those around a mourner cannot cope with the mourner's grief but the diagnosis of chronic grief should *only* be made by a specialist.

3 Other factors contributing to pathological grief

We could find several other reasons that contribute to the fail-ure to resolve grief. Some authors have identified up to fifty! We mentioned earlier how what is happening at the time of the death and the circumstances of the death itself greatly influence the resolution of grief. We have seen how sudden, violent, unexpected or untimely deaths increase the risk of abnormal grief. One factor is considered of vital importance by most authors, both Christians and non-Christians; *beliefs*. The power of faith in the course of grief is so outstanding that we need to devote a whole chapter to it. It is enough to quote here the words of an expert in a secular book: 'One of the most frequently used and effective means of coping with death has been through the survivor's faith, their belief in God.'[23] Now we will turn to two other factors, existing before the death, which are decisive in the course of the bereavement.

---

[23] Stephen R. Shuchter, *Handbook of Bereavement*, (Cambridge: Cambridge University Press, 1993) 32

- The personality of the person grieving.
- The kind of relationship they had with the deceased.

Personality problems

Our personality is a powerful factor in the prognosis of grief – whether we recover from it or not. There is a clear relationship between them. A healthy personality will eventually lead to the resolution of grief, in the stages we considered normal. On the other hand, personality problems are a risk factor for the outcome of bereavement. The obvious question then is: what kind of personality problems are we talking about? What is it that makes some of us more vulnerable in the grief process?

Some authors, especially in the eighties, claimed that those people characterised by feelings of inadequacy, insecurity, fearfulness or inferiority were more prone to pathological grief. So, according to them, both depressive and anxious personalities had an increased risk. Likewise we considered earlier how those unable to control or express their feelings would probably suffer from an inhibited grief.

Today, more importance is given to the so-called attachment theory. It claims that personality development is very much influenced by the kind of emotional bond built during childhood with our key figures, our mother and father. This early attachment is like the language that we speak later on in all our relationships, especially the closest ones. Our relationships as adults reflect the same pattern that we learnt as children. There are basically three different types of attachment: anxious attachment, insecure attachment and secure attachment. In the case of anxious and insecure attachments to parents, children develop a personality characterised by great dependency (a dependent personality disorder, as we will consider in our next point). They feel devastated or helpless when close relationships end and are frequently preoccupied with fears of being abandoned.

We need not to go into detail about the psychology of these emotional links. It is enough to know that the way we related to our loving figures in childhood will clearly influence our response to loss; not only in the case of death, but to any loss in general. In these cases, group support is very important because it becomes the key which allows these people to overcome the extra weight that grief means in their burdened personality.

The previous relationship to the deceased

There are mainly two situations when the relationship between the mourner and the loved one who dies will affect the quality of the grief.

- Very dependent relationships
- Ambivalent relationships

● *Dependent relationships*
Excessive *dependency* is the key problem that explains most cases of chronic grief. In this sense, chronic grief, rather than being an evidence of love, is usually the result of severe and crippling dependency. What do we mean by excessive dependency? What is the difference between a healthy close relationship and neurotic dependency? Neurotic dependency occurs when one person, in an unequal relationship, feels like a child and views the other one as the adult protective figure. For some reasons, the pair chose not to grow emotionally. This 'Peter Pan syndrome' is easy to identify from sentences such as: 'I can't do without them. I wouldn't be able to survive if they died' (this is a literal quotation from one of my patients, aged thirty, referring to both of her parents).

Dependent people do not develop an identity of their own, but they borrow it from their loved ones. So when the loved ones die, the dependent person feel a complete loss of self, which becomes a devastating and unbearable experience. In fact, the loss is two-fold: they have lost not only the loved person, but the identity they rented from them. Sometimes this can lead to suicide attempts and depression is quite common. Dependent people feel totally unsheltered in this world. In this context, widows can be a group of high risk, especially if they are young, have small children, without relatives nearby and were financially dependent on their late husbands.

The same effects (but for the opposite reason) may occur when the survivor is the protective – or adult – part of the dependent relationship. This is why a prolonged mourning is understandable and almost normal in the case of a parent who has lost a child because the personality of a small child is always like an extension of that of its parents. When the child dies, it is like losing part of yourself.

> I felt like I had had a leg amputated and I was having to learn to walk without my other leg – I've got to learn to live again but I don't know how to do this because I have never been this way before.[24]

Sometimes the problem in the relationship comes not so much from the dependency itself, but from its exclusiveness. Close relationships with others do not exist: the pair have no friends, no social life; the relationship revolves entirely around themselves. No wonder then, that absolute loneliness and difficult grief are the outcome when one of the two passes away. This is something quite usual in the grief caused by divorce. An intimate relationship, and marriage is the most intimate one, should not develop at the expense of all other friendships. The local church provides Christians with a wonderful framework to cultivate strong relationships (see chapter 3). Clubs and societies, family networks and friendships can also provide similar support from a social viewpoint.

- *Ambivalent relationships*

Ambivalence is the presence of positive and negative feelings towards a loved person at the same time. Love and hate, affection and rejection, a desire to draw near and to separate, all occur simultaneously. A small degree of ambivalence is a universal phenomenon and would not be considered pathological.

---

[24] Peter Reynolds, Interview, October 2003

The problem for some people comes when the negative feelings have been very strong. Either consciously or not, they hated the deceased to such an extent that this causes guilt, as we saw earlier. If this hostility is not resolved while the person is still alive, a pathological grief is very likely to happen.

Sometimes it is not so much a matter of something being wrong with the mourner themselves, but simply of problems in the relationship prior to the death. The quality of the relationship will determine to a great extent the health of the bereavement. It is logical to suppose that those who relate poorly to the living are going to relate poorly to the dead. When the relationship between the mourner and the deceased had problems, it is very likely that some kind of emotional problems will persist after the loss. Siblings who have not talked for years, parents and children who did not relate at all, sometimes not meeting for twenty years or more; family conflicts that remain unresolved or simply love that was not shown properly – all these will probably lead to difficulties in grieving. It is so important that we keep our relationships as healthy as possible while we still have the chance! This is the best antidote to pathological grief and it leads us naturally to a vital theme: the prevention of grief.

The prevention of grief

An old proverb says that 'prevention is better than cure.' Can we apply this principle to our subject? In what sense can we anticipate grief, in order to be better prepared to face death when it comes? Anticipatory grief is an important phase of bereavement because it allows emotional preparation and thus makes the adjustment easier. Grieving in advance is useful for both the pre-mourners and the person facing death. It is not an easy task because no one likes to think of death or separation before it actually comes. We all prefer to postpone thinking of these undesired events, especially in our society where death is almost a taboo. The expectation of death permits rehearsal and enables survivors to realise death as a possibility before it actually comes. This diminishes the risk of overwhelming stress. It is very unusual to see pathological grief reactions when there was a good preparatory work.

We find a good example of this principle in the life of King David. The child that was born as the result of the sinful relationship with Bathsheba fell very sick. 'David pleaded with God for the child. He fasted and went into his house and spent the nights lying on the ground. The elders of his household stood beside him to get him up from the ground, but he refused, and he would not eat any food with them' (2 Sam.12:15-17).

Here we find David suffering the symptoms typical of acute mourning. Actually the child had not died yet, but he *anticipated* the grief. He wisely and promptly did all that he could humanly do to save the child: he prayed, he fasted, he remained awake, etc. David's reaction was probably an intuitive one, but with his behaviour he was planting the seeds for a healthy grief some days later. Indeed, something happened which seemed very strange to the servants

> On the seventh day the child died. David's servants were afraid to tell him that the child was dead, for they thought, 'While the child was still living, we spoke to David but he would not listen to us. How can we tell him the child is dead? He may do something desperate.' David noticed that his servants were whispering among themselves and he realised that the child was dead. 'Is the child dead?' he asked. 'Yes,' they replied, 'he is dead.' Then David got up from the ground. After he had washed, put on lotions and changed his clothes, he went into the house of the LORD and worshipped. Then he went to his own house, and at his request they served him food, and he ate. His servants asked him, 'Why are you acting this way? While the child was alive, you fasted and wept, but now that the child is dead, you get up and eat!' (2 Sam. 12:18-21)

The answer David gave them is an outstanding lesson in anticipatory grief: 'While the child was still alive, I fasted and wept.

I thought, "Who knows? The LORD may be gracious to me and let the child live." But now that he is dead, why should I fast? Can I bring him back again?' (2 Sam.12:22,23a).

We can notice the positive effects of anticipatory grief on David by his readiness to comfort Bathsheba (v. 24), the mother of the child who was no doubt in great sorrow. David had the emotional and spiritual strength to give himself to his new wife because he had done an excellent preparation for grief. Notice, incidentally, the deep insight he had on the nature of death as a transient stage, when he says with great serenity: 'I will go to him, but he will not return to me' (v. 23). This is a beautiful way to express the hope of a future reunion and an example of how faith dramatically changes our perspective on death.

Of course, anticipatory grief can only be done in those cases when you see death approaching, that is sickness and old age. In the Old Testament we see some of the patriarchs following a tradition which contains a lot of wisdom: the blessing by the father of the children and grandchildren before dying. This ritual, quite normal in ancient Jewish families, displays very healthy attitudes for the prevention of grief. It gives a unique opportunity for intimate communication, when words never said before are pronounced; it allows the warm expression of love which a near farewell always stimulates.

Let us take the case of Jacob as an example.

> When the time drew near for Israel (Jacob) to die, he called for his son Joseph and said to him, 'If I have found favour in your eyes, put your hand under my thigh and promise that you will show me kindness and faithfulness. Do not bury me in Egypt, but when I rest with my fathers ... bury me where they are buried.' 'I will do as you say,' he said ... Israel worshipped as he leaned on the top of his staff. (Gen. 47:29-31).

At this first step, father and son are solving some practical 'business' related to the burial. They are not embarrassed by the nearness of death and they speak about it in a strikingly natural way.

A bit later, it is Joseph who takes the initiative as he hears of the worsening of his father's health (48:1) and brings his two sons, Manasseh and Ephraim, to Jacob in order to receive their grandfather's blessing.

> When Jacob was told, 'Your son Joseph has come to you,' Israel rallied his strength and sat up on the bed ... When Israel saw the sons of Joseph, he asked 'Who are these?' 'They are the sons God has given me here,' Joseph said to his father. Then Israel said, 'Bring them to me so that I may bless them.' Now Israel's eyes were failing because of old age, and he could hardly see. So Joseph brought his sons close to him, and his father kissed them and embraced them (Gen. 48:2,8,9).

Such an expression of love through intimate words, kissing and embracing is the best antidote against pathological grief. It is a most natural way to anticipate grief and prepare everything for a normal bereavement.

One final remark about Jacob's last days as a good example in the prevention of grief: the importance of being together with the loved one when they die. 'Then Jacob called for his sons and said: "Gather round so that I can tell you what will happen to you in the days to come ... Assemble and listen ... listen to your father ..."' (49:1,2). Later we read: 'When Jacob had finished giving instructions to his sons, he drew his feet up into the bed, breathed his last and was gathered to his people. Joseph threw himself upon his father and wept over him and kissed him' (49:33 – 50:1).

We have a similar example in Paul's farewell to the Ephesian elders: 'When [Paul] had said this, he knelt down with all of them and they prayed. They all wept as they embraced him and kissed him. What grieved them most was his statement that they would never see his face again.' (Acts 20:36-38).

These moving records show how important it is, both for the dying person and for the bereaved, to experience the warmth of physical nearness in their last moments. This is one of the most relieving things for the bereaved. Time and again in my

conversations with mourners, having been present by the bedside in the very moment of death makes a healthy difference: 'We
held hands as he passed away and we prayed together,' shared a
widow, with a ray of bright joy in her eyes. It is said that Johann
S. Bach, the great musician who was a committed Christian, died
surrounded by all his children – some of them musicians too –
singing and playing one of his father's favourite pieces.
Unfortunately a reunion of the whole family is not always
possible for various reasons. Though this is not our subject here,
we as Christians should claim a more human, less 'technical',
way of dying. Being at home when death comes, surrounded by
your loved ones, is probably the best anticipation for the great
reunion in the Home par excellence, heaven.

We would like to close this section with some suggestions
on preventing grief and thus facing bereavement in the least
painful way. In your relationship with your loved ones:

- Do not take love for granted. Express it openly whenever
  you have an opportunity.
- Thank the loved one now for all they do and mean in your
  life, for all they give you.
- Ask what you can do for them now. Remember the essence of
  love, according to Jesus (the Golden Rule in Matthew 7:12).
- Finish your 'homework' with the loved one. Try to talk and
  resolve those unfinished matters which have been on the
  waiting list for years – sort out anything that needs forgiving, on either side.
- Avoid tensions or quarrels as much as possible, don't use
  nasty or harsh words with those you love, and resolve dis-
  agreements or agree to disagree.
- Keep the relationship as peaceful as possible. Peace and
  health are closely related concepts in the Bible.
- Enjoy the relationship now and live in the present. Praise
  God that you have the one you love with you.

When I was a teenager, I 'discovered' a short anonymous
poem that my father had hanging on one of the walls of his
library at home. Its content inspired me for many years and

became a challenge in my relationships. I especially tried to apply it to my loved ones. Today, thirty years later, I can tell you that the efforts to put it into practice have been the best investment I could ever make.

> Only once I shall pass through this world
> if there is any word of goodness
> that I can pronounce;
> any noble deed that I can make
> may I say this word, may I make this deed now
> since I shall not pass through here anymore[25]

* * *

Chris Anderson[26] suffered three bereavements over an eight year period – leaving him without any close blood relatives. Grieving was difficult and complicated.

My father died unexpectedly suddenly in 1988. He was sixty-four and I half his age. They were on holiday in Portugal; we had just started a holiday in France. My older (and only) brother died suddenly in 1994 – he was forty-one. He had been ill with pneumonia but we didn't know. He was discovered dead by a passer-by outside the pub near where he lived. Mother died in 1996 after suffering heart failure for a gruelling three months.

After my father died, I was shocked, stunned, disbelieving. My sister-in-law rang to tell us. She said 'Your father had a heart attack and died.' I felt 'That can't be right. People have heart attacks and get a second chance; they only die when they've had heart problems for a while...' Irrational logic.

My main thought was how to support my mum. That saved me from having to think too much. She was remarkably calm and looked well. I thought this was good, but didn't realise that she was just protected by the initial shock. I think when someone dies those really close to the dead person go into shock, which is in some sense unreal,

---

[25] Source unknown
[26] Not his real name

but in many ways a blessing. They actually act and behave much calmer and more rationally than others who may be less shocked. It's only later that the grief and pain comes out.

This shock effect can be quite disorienting for others. They expect those closest to fall apart, but they don't. As a result the close ones appear to give out the message that they're OK, support is not required. And later when the grief really hits them (after say three months) and they start to be able to feel in the way others less close immediately felt, then there is nobody there.

I spent a lot of time from then on supporting my mother – handling the funeral and acting as executor. There was no time for me to grieve. Spiritually I was numb, emotionally shocked and physically tired from sleeplessness and stress.

Spiritually I felt that God was guiding my life in this way and it was something I had to go through with. It was a mentally draining experience as I had to drop everything and help my mother sort things out. You can't hear God when you are ill or stressed in this sort of situation, unless he shouts at you. And he doesn't tend to do that. So you keep navigating on autopilot, knowing he is there but not being in touch.

My mother died after a traumatic period of suffering progressive heart failure. There were midnight dashes to the hospital having been told she might not be alive when I got there, only to find her happy and smiling when I arrived. Then there were the hours of sitting at her bedside. The worst aspect was that the later stages of the illness affected her personality and that made it doubly difficult. There was the responsibility of agreeing with the consultant not to resuscitate if things went wrong. And then the guilt of lying to my mum when she asked if she was going to recover. That changed my perception of God's view of lying and deceit.

My mother died on the one weekend in three months when we decided we just needed to go away somewhere for a break. I think God was in the timing, but to be honest by the time she died I was emotionally exhausted and hardly capable of complex or even rational thought. I was just a psychological billiard ball cannoning off anything I came across with no real control. Suddenly I was alone and carrying the responsibility of sorting everything else. Responsibility is lonely and being the last of a family makes it worse.

The main thing I felt after all this was a sense of having been robbed of any opportunity to grieve for my family. With the first two deaths I had to look after my mum rather than allow myself space to grieve, and then when she died I was just too exhausted to be able to grieve properly. The real benefits that came out of it were to do with being able to help others who are bereaved. You never get over bereavement, and it annoys me when people say 'he'll soon get over it'. You don't get over it, you just learn to accept it and it becomes part of you. And grief is funny. It doesn't tend to come when you expect it. Talking to someone about the dead person generally doesn't bring it on. It just comes out at odd moments and bites your ankles when you least expect it. Almost anything can trigger it. The obvious triggers don't tend to, I guess because you know they are there and are prepared for them.

You shouldn't ignore or avoid someone who is grieving – they don't change and become a pariah just because a loved one is dead. Often it can be very helpful if they are asked about their own feelings about the dead person, or just how they are coping. People like talking about the dead person, and like being treated sensitively but normally.

Grieving goes on for a very long time and it is helpful to be concerned about their grief even years after the death. Save your special card for three months after the death when everyone else has forgotten, and if you send a card on the anniversary of the death, that helps enormously to say you care.

Other things that are helpful are memories and mementos of the dead person. Memories shared in writing can help as these can be kept and saved for later when they make more sense. These can help the grieving person build a better picture of the person they have lost, at a time when they are having to rely just on their own memories for the first time.

I think my greatest sense of loss is that of memories. I have nobody now to reminisce with, to share memories of what has gone. And there is a feeling of memories slipping away, falling down a cliff when you are trying to hold on with slippery hands.

Then there is the loneliness. Nobody shares your experiences and values more than the nuclear family that you grow up with, yet for me these are gone. I'm close to my wife and daughter, but they are different and I am the last vessel of a previous age which is so impor-

tant to me. I am alone. If I can't remember nobody can. And there is
no one to remind me.

I've helped myself by giving myself space on my own, by the family graves perhaps, or near their old home, and letting tears come if
they want to. I speak to them and God and tell them how lonely and
alone I feel, and how much I loved them, and how I try to live the life
they would have liked me to. I also tell them about my daughter and
how she is growing up. I know they can't hear, but it helps because I
am expressing myself. My father never knew my daughter and they
would have loved each other so much: they have just the right personalities for each other.

God hears too. I often feel I know a bit how Job felt. There is the
offer of restoration... but how long will the wait be? Sometimes I feel
if God takes any more then there will be nothing left.

3

How can we help?

comforting the bereaved

'I would like to help a close friend of mine who lost his brother in an accident, but I feel very embarrassed in these kind of
situations; I don't know what to say or do. I'm afraid that my
words may be more a nuisance than a real support. Please,
how can I be a real help?' This request, shared by a young man
in a letter, is a good summary of the difficulties many people
have when they face a mourning person. They just do not
know how to approach them.

It is very obvious that the comfort of relatives, friends and
other close people is one of the key factors for the normal
development of grief. It is an invaluable instrument to help the
bereaved cope with their sorrow. Mourners can feel very cut
off from those around them, while at the same time needing
their company and dreading being alone. Many of those inter-
viewed for this book remembered with gratitude those who
had taken the time to come and see them. So if the support of
others is so vital, we need to know how to implement it for the
benefit of the afflicted.

With this purpose in mind we will consider three basic
questions.

- What are the needs of the bereaved? – What is expected
  from us

- What are the mistakes we should avoid? – What we should not do or say
- When is it the right moment? – Appropriate timing for the different kinds of help

Before we deal with these questions, one practical point must be clarified: *who* can help? Are some people more suitable than others to provide care for the bereaved? Research has shown that the first source of support comes from the family and the closest friends, especially in the first days. The presence of a spouse, daughter, son, father or mother, as well as intimate friends is most appreciated by the mourner and becomes a source of major comfort. Likewise, their absence is remembered negatively for a long time: 'You were not there the day we buried him' comes as a bitter rebuke. Hence the reunion of the whole family is a priority, even for those who did not get along very well. On such occasions any tension or difference of opinion should be subordinated to the main purpose: supporting the grieving person with your presence.

Secondly, those people who went through a similar experience before are very helpful: for example a young widow can find great relief in sharing with another young widow; they should understand each other well because they face similar feelings or problems and there is a mutual spontaneous sympathy. This often applies especially to parents who have lost a child and to those whose loved ones died in traumatic circumstances. Thirdly, the support of the clergy and 'religious groups' – in our case, the local church – has proved to be highly valued. We will consider later on in more detail how the church can help in grieving situations. Let us simply say that when the church really functions as a spiritual family, then its support for the afflicted is certainly meaningful.

One principle is clear and universally accepted: most mourners need no counselling because normal grief requires no professional or specialised help. This way, comforting comes before counselling; the warmth of the loved ones before the skill of the professional. Except for the cases of pathological grief, you do not need a degree in psychology or to be a trained counsellor to help someone mourning. It is a process of healing where following the rules of common sense should be enough. However, support groups – particularly for those who have lost children or life partners – can be enormously helpful and details of some relevant organisations can be found at the back of the book.

But you may wonder: is it really that easy? The problem comes because many people, including members of the caring professions, are not emotionally ready to face death personally. For this reason they make mistakes which interfere with the grieving process. For example, they feel very embarrassed when the bereaved cries and try to mask the pain of the moment with sentences such as 'He is in a better place' or 'She isn't suffering any more', which are true but not helpful. Those who are supposed to help may become an obstacle. We should remember here the old Latin dictum referring to doctors: *primum non nocere*, which means 'the most important thing is not to harm' and apply it to all those who try to comfort a grieving person.

The needs of the bereaved

The first step when you want to help someone is to be aware of their needs, either emotional, spiritual or material ones. The same principle applies to the grieving person. We have chosen here the needs we consider essential for the resolution of grief. Many others could be mentioned, but we do not want our readers to get lost in a diffused 'forest' of suggestions. This is why we summarise them in four sections. Each one of these main needs correlates roughly with the different states of normal grief. We believe such correspondence will help you to relate the symptoms described in chapter 1, that is the realities which you will find in your contact with the bereaved, with the proper attitudes to have. We would like it become a kind of road map to help our readers drive adequately through the bendy roads of bereavement.

- Support – numbness
- Emotional expression – acute mourning
- Understanding – loneliness and withdrawal
- Reorganisation – adaptation

Each of these needs can also be present in some degree during the other phases. In grief nothing happens in closed compartments, and many of its phenomena are often recurrent.

1 Support

The need for support lasts for the whole process of grief, but it reaches a peak in the first days and weeks when it is felt very intensely. How can we express support to the grieving person? We could mention many ways, but for practical purposes we shall group them in three main suggestions.

Be there. To be there alongside the mourner in their suffering is the first and most elementary step in the process of helping. Why? Being there is a natural way to express sympathy or compassion. Both words mean the same thing: 'to suffer together with' and they are the core of the healing of any emotional wounds. Actually this is what Paul encouraged us to do in one of the most beautiful chapters of the New Testament: '… mourn with those who mourn' (Rom.12:15). The lack of compassionate people willing to suffer together with the bereaved clearly worsens the course of grief. Loneliness then becomes an unbearable burden.

Being alongside, our presence, conveys a message which has no substitute: 'I am with you, I am for you.' It is a supreme way to communicate love. I once went to visit the parents of a young man who had been killed in a road accident on that very day. Several months later they said to me: 'Thank you for being with us. Your presence made a great difference to us.' Here we find a most important principle: the main need of the grieving person is not words, but warmth. And in grief warmth is better expressed with the language of gestures: an arm round their shoulders or a kiss speak far more clearly than any words can, and reach directly to the heart. Non-verbal communication of support is a powerful way to show how much we care for others.

This close connection between being present and comforting is beautifully portrayed in the narrative of the resurrection of Lazarus. Three times we find a sentence which refers to the presence of the friends and neighbours of the village: 'many ... had *come* to Martha and Mary to *comfort* them' (Jn. 11:19); 'When the Jews who *had been with* Mary in the house, *comforting* her ...' (v. 31); 'When Jesus saw [Mary] weeping and the Jews who *had come along* with her also weeping' (v. 33 – all authors' emphasis). Notice the close connection in verses 19 and 31 between their 'coming to, being with' and comforting. The very fact of being there with the two grieving sisters was a way of comforting them. Comfort is received primarily not through words, but through closeness. It is interesting to notice that the word 'to assist' – which means to give help, to take care of – comes from a Latin word whose literal translation is 'to be alongside, to be together with.'

I remember the funeral of a man who died in his early fifties from a heart attack. He was a good friend of my family so the widow asked me to preach at the funeral service. I prepared the message thoroughly because it was a good opportunity to witness to our faith. I knew that many people would attend, including the local authorities as he was a popular man in the town. Just a few days later, the widow told me: 'Thank you very much. I was not able to pay attention to your message; I could not concentrate at all so I do not even know what you preached about, but thank you very much for *being there with us*.' I will never forget her words.

One practical point which is often neglected: how long should you be alongside and available? Some people believe that the mourner needs support only for the first few days. This is a very common mistake. *Do not stop your help too early*. After the initial stage of numbness, the bereaved becomes fully aware of the reality and it is then, when everybody goes back home after the funeral, that loneliness is felt most intensely. The need of company is certainly more intense in the first two weeks, but it actually goes far beyond this initial period. As someone said, 'the first two years are, at least, as important as the first two weeks.'[27]

Hence the need to continue our attentions to show that we do not forget them. If you are not available for a personal visit, little tokens of affection such as a phone call, lending a book, writing a postcard or a letter, sending a little gift, all of them are highly appreciated. They convey an important message: 'We haven't forgotten you: we are here with you.' We must be flexible regarding the frequency of contact because each person is different from others, but I would suggest that once a week is not too much during the first three months, specially if the mourner is a close friend or relative. Also be alert on special occasions like anniversaries and holidays, when the absence of the loved one is felt very intensely.

Don't say too much. 'I don't like visiting those who are grieving, because I don't know what to say,' a young girl told me. 'If you feel this way, probably you are the right person to go!' I replied. She looked very surprised and inquired why. Her belief reflects a common mistake: some people think that support should be expressed with words. The reality is quite the opposite: in bereavement, as in many other situations of suffering, *we are not called to preach, but to sympathise.* The grieving person does not need the eloquence of a long discourse, but the warmth of a caring hand.

> It would have been helpful if people had let me talk, even if I did want to go over the same things again and again. But mainly those I met were more concerned about their own reactions and were afraid of having to struggle with me. So they just got away as soon as they could – or else told me long stories of their own grief, their own losses.[28]

---

[27] Joyce Landorf, *Mourning song* (Baker Book House: New Jersey, 1974), 145

[28] Maggie, Interview, 2003

The author of Ecclesiastes was very wise when he wrote: 'There is a time for everything … a time to be silent and a time to speak' (Ecc. 3:1a,7b). The early stages of grief are mostly a time to be silent. If we feel that we should speak, then our words, as the apostle Paul remind us, should be 'always full of grace, seasoned with salt' (Col. 4:6). The example of Jesus on the cross is remarkable. One short sentence to the thief crucified by his side was enough: 'I tell you the truth, today you will be with me in paradise' (Lk. 23:43). This sentence contained all the comfort that the thief needed: a soothing word of hope. Jesus did not preach to him; he did not use many words or elaborate an 'evangelistic message' to the dying one. He just said what the thief needed to hear. The Lord showed great wisdom and sensitivity any time he dealt with the afflicted ones in his earthly life.

Joe Bayly, who lost three sons in different circumstances, a real 'man of sorrows and familiar with suffering', wrote on a certain occasion during one of his periods of grief: 'I remember once, I was sitting torn into pieces by sharp pain, when someone came in and started talking about God's plans, about the "why" that death happened, about the hope beyond the grave. He went on talking, telling me things which I knew well enough that were true. Nevertheless, I remained quiet, without any other emotion than the desire that he left as soon as possible. He finally did. Another person came then and he sat down by my side. He did not ask me any question. He simply remained sitting near me for more than one hour, he listened when I said something, he replied briefly, he prayed shortly. I felt moved. And comforted. When he left I felt really sorry.'

Be sensitive, choose your words carefully and remember that in times of suffering words may be silver, but silence is golden. Talking too much was the mistake made by the friends of Job. Initially they did the right thing: 'They sat on the ground with him for seven days and seven nights. No-one said a word to him, because they saw how great his suffering was' (Job 2:13). It is a pity that they did not remain silent because as soon as they started speaking, they talked nonsense. This was the reason why God rebuked them at the end of the story: 'I am angry with you and your two friends, because you have not *spoken* of me what is right, as my servant Job has' (Job 42:7 – authors' emphasis). If they had remained silent, their support to the tormented Job would have been much more efficient.

Do not feel embarrassed by the periods of silence, even long ones. The Russian writer Chekov, who himself went through a lot of suffering in his life, said: 'When happiness and misery are extreme, they can only be expressed properly through silence.' These times of silence are fruitful because they contain a great therapeutic potential. It is in the quietness of silence that you can listen to your inner voices, you can reflect upon unusual thoughts, you can clarify your feelings, and above all when you can encounter God: 'Be still, and know that I am God' (Ps. 46:10). The Almighty often speaks to us in seasons of sorrow when the heart is shaken by the 'earthquakes' of life. The silence and quietness of grief are necessary to be able to hear his voice. And be ready to listen – we will cover this more fully later on in the section on understanding.

Be available for practical things. This is another way to give support: to provide practical help. Each one of us has different gifts; for those with the gift of 'exhortation' – which is not preaching, but comforting – the two first forms of support mentioned so far will be very appropriate. But some people find dealing with feelings too threatening. They feel embarrassed, in part because they have a different gift, the gift of 'service'. For such persons there is also an opportunity to help. What can they do? A lot of practical tasks need to be performed in the first hours and days: the funeral arrangements, the bureaucratic steps for the burial, preparing meals, taking care of the children, and so on. Offer to do what you can see needs doing, don't wait to be asked.

> One of the things that hurt us most was somebody – who was in leadership – sent a card, which said 'Let us know if there is anything we can do to help.' This is the stupidest thing to say

to a bereaved parent. You can't think what you need – you never give them a call. You're hurting too much.[29]

Being relieved from stressful busyness at this stage will allow the bereaved to concentrate their energy on the expression of grief. A friend of mine lost his father some years ago, when we were both students. I offered myself to write the death notice and the programme for the service. This task may take some time because you have to go to the printing house and supervise many details. After 25 years, my friend is still so grateful for this small practical help, that he mentioned several times what it meant to him: 'Your help allowed me to take care of my mother and sister.' So when we tell the bereaved 'do not worry about doing so and so, I will do it for you,' we are giving practical support which is greatly appreciated.

2. Emotional expression

The bereaved has a natural need to release the effects related to the loss. This happens mainly, though not exclusively, during the second stage, when the pangs of pain are so acute and painful. Their intense yearning to reunite with the loved one and the profound sense of loss require an outlet which relieves their disturbing feelings, specially anger, confusion, guilt and pain. This process is called catharsis (a word used in psychology which literally means 'purging'). It is freely to pour out, without any restrictions, what we feel. All that we may do to contribute to this emotional expression will be healing to the bereaved.

Therefore, we have a two-fold task here.

- We must let them know that their expression of feelings is acceptable to God and good for themselves
- We must facilitate, though not pressure, this emotional expression

[29] Peter and Barbie Reynolds, Interview, 2003

Before we consider this two-fold goal, we return to an idea we introduced in the beginning of this chapter: it is very important for the family *to be* together, physically near. But it is equally important that the family *grieves together*. They must talk openly about their thoughts, share their feelings, cry together: parents with children, spouses with each other, brothers with sisters. It is sad when the members of the family are reluctant to show their feelings to the rest of the members; then each one grieves alone and in their own way. If this happens, the seeds are sown for later family difficulties, some of which may be serious. Grieving separately is very dangerous for the family life as well as for yourself. Certainly no one can grieve *for you*; in this sense it is an individual process. But grief has also a body dimension which is necessary for its resolution. Hence the great therapeutic value of the family grieving together. We will go back to this idea when we refer to the role of the church, our spiritual family. We should also point out that people often grieve in very different ways, so don't be surprised by this.

Different ways to express emotions

How can we accomplish this two-fold goal? First of all, we should notice that there are no fixed clichés as far as pouring out our deepest feelings. We are all different and each one of us has a natural way to release the sorrow in their heart. The outpouring of tears or anger obviously makes for a good catharsis. But there are other excellent ways.

Some people are able to *verbalise* their feelings, and others even prefer to *write* them down as their capacity to put grief into words is remarkable. This was the case of C.S. Lewis in *A grief observed*, and also of Richard Baxter, a prominent pastor and preacher in the seventeenth century who wrote *A Breviary* a few weeks after his wife Margaret died. This little book, in the words of J. Packer, contains 'an object lesson in what we may properly call grief management. Here we shall meet a grieving husband memorialising the soulmate whom, after nineteen years of marriage, he had tragically lost at the age of forty-five.'[30] Likewise, a good number of current books on bereavement are personal testimonies which show the need for self expression during the grief process.

Even if you are not planning to publish it, it is helpful to keep a journal linking events and feelings together from day to day. It helps to clarify the confusion inside, to express despair or doubts, to reflect on the guilt feelings, to pour out the anger or hostility. You can share and talk about this writing regularly with a friend or a counsellor and it can be a great relief.

Why do we express grieving feelings in various ways? Several reasons explain such differences. Sometimes it has to do with temperament; the introvert person is much less prone to show feelings than extrovert one.[31] Also our upbringing: those who were brought up in homes with a lot of emotional expression will find it easier than those who lived in an environment of emotional deprivation and inhibition. Even cultural factors have a lot to do in this matter: it is a well-known fact that certain countries and cultures, for example in the East, promote a lot of public expression of feelings in bereavement. Hence the presence of the old figure of the professional mourner – usually women – whose task was precisely to encourage weeping, both at the house of the deceased and at the funeral.

> As a family we all coped in different ways. Certainly in the first few days, my sister didn't want to talk to anybody, but to me it helped to talk to anybody and everybody, so whenever the phone rang, I would answer it because I wanted to talk about my dad. I was the one who went shopping because every time we walked up the street, people would stop and talk to me. Whereas I know for my sister and my mum, they couldn't face people. And for me it helped other people saying how much

---

[30] J.I Packer, *A grief sanctified*, (Leicester: Crossway Books, 1998), 12-13

[31] For further study of this topic – how the temperament influences our spiritual and emotional life – see the book *Prayer: how your personality affects the way you pray*, Pablo Martinez, (Carlisle: Spring Harvest Publishing Division and Authentic Lifestyle, 2001)

they appreciated him, what a shock it was ... that other people shared, to some extent, how I felt.[32]

The value of grieving rituals

Grieving rituals play an important role in the expression of feelings. Actually a lot of the catharsis is done during the burial ceremonies because they are perceived as the last 'goodbye'. Such a perception often acts like a trigger point for the outpouring of tears or other feelings. For some people who find the expression of feelings really difficult, this may be the only time when they weep and openly express their pain. 'I couldn't cry, not before the funeral nor afterwards, but during the service and all the ceremonies, I couldn't stop crying' said a man who hardly ever expresses any feeling.

We should encourage, therefore, the bereaved to participate in the funeral, memorial service or any other ritual because they are a great help to make the fact of the death more real – remember the state of numbness usually finishes abruptly after the funeral – and they provide excellent opportunities to experience the solidarity and sympathy of friends and the community. The grieving rituals in all cultures are a valuable means of stimulating the work of mourning. We should not take their value for granted.

What about the visits to the cemetery? Are they useless? Are they wrong? Visiting a grave site is a sign of remembrance. In this sense it can help the bereaved express feelings, remember and come to terms with reality, so they are not useless. Normally the need to go to the cemetery diminishes with time. Only a strong desire to go often, especially after the first year, can reveal a morbid preoccupation near to pathological grief. Therefore you should not stop the bereaved person visiting the grave, but nor should you force them to do so. There are many other ways to remember the loved one which are emotionally healing.

---

[32] Sarah Peacock, Interview, 2003

There are still people who even now will think to phone us on an anniversary, or at least mention an anniversary. They haven't forgotten any more than we have.[33]

There are some *mistakes* we may make regarding the emotional expression. We must be aware of the most common ones and avoid them.

Minimising the feelings

This is to diminish the depth or intensity of the loss. Sentences such as: 'Do not cry; he is better now, he is with the Lord' are not helpful. They trivialise the pain of the separation. Let us remember that death, though a universal phenomenon, is not natural at all because we were not created to die. We do not find a single situation in the New Testament, either in Jesus' ministry or in the apostolic times, where the sorrow or pain caused by death is minimised. The exhortation to 'weep with those who weep' (Rom. 12:15, RSV) suggests the opposite.

Special attention should be given to the expression of anger and guilt, two of the most prevalent reactions in the second stage of bereavement. We must manage such feelings in a sensitive way. In the case of anger we should not condemn or argue about it. Just listen. All that the bereaved needs to know at this point is that hostility is a normal feature of the grief process and, therefore, it is understood by our merciful and compassionate God. It will disappear as time passes by. Gently remind them how many of the great servants of God eventually went through periods of much anger towards God: and yet they did not sin, neither were they rebuked for their feelings. As we said earlier, anger can become a sin when it gives place to bitterness, which leads to a persistent, long-lasting resentment against God or others. So our task as helpers is simply to overview the course of anger and be watchful that it is not turned into bitterness.

---

[33] Ali Risbridger, Interview, 2000

In the case of *guilt*, remember the comments made in chapter 1. The main relief for the mourner comes from discovering that such feelings do not correlate to any real mistake, it has no foundation whatsoever, but it is an unconscious way to express the pain of the separation. Our goal is to reassure the bereaved that they did everything possible for the lost one. In this sense it is good to review together in detail the last weeks or months and help them notice how supportive and caring they were for the deceased. I encourage my patients to do this review exercise in the form of a written list. 'Write down all the specific good things you did for them in the last months. Also think of some aspect that, in your opinion, you neglected which makes you feel guilty.' The results are often a surprise to them because they get an objective panorama of the excellent care they gave the loved one and they realise how distorted their conclusions were. When the guilt becomes obsessive it may hide a depression and require the intervention of a specialist. If you suspect this happening, try gently to encourage the bereaved to visit their GP.

Discouraging the expression of feelings

Feelings are not negative in themselves. We were created with emotions and we all need to express such emotions. The fact that the Fall, that is the entrance of sin in the world, affected this area of our personality does not mean that we should repress feelings as much as possible. We must gently, but firmly, convince the bereaved that this is not a biblical idea. Jesus, our model in all our behaviour, never suppressed either his own emotions or those of the suffering people.

Let us go back to the text when the Lord was deeply moved and wept before the tomb of Lazarus. If Jesus knew that his friend would come to life in just a few moments, why did he weep? Is it not a striking reaction, somehow surprising, when he was fully aware of the event that would follow, that is Lazarus' resurrection? The answer is an important one: Jesus was fully human and the emotional impact of the situation was such that he could not avoid these tears. I am convinced

that the Holy Spirit provided us with this memorable passage
not only as a sign of Jesus' humanity and sensitivity, but also
as a reminder that – following his example – we should not
repress the expression of grief either. Learning to weep without shame is an important step in the grief pathway.

The two mistakes just mentioned usually spring from the
same source: the fact that most people tend to feel very
embarrassed before certain feelings, specially tears. As soon
as someone starts weeping, our automatic reaction is to try to
stop them. This can be more about protecting ourselves from
their pain, rather than coming from a real desire to help the
bereaved. Supporting the bereaved is painful and we need to
recognise that but not run away from it. It is almost a condi-
tioned reflex: 'Don't cry' we say and we quickly improvise
any reason to justify our attitude. If we understood how
helpful these tears are and how much they contribute to the
healing of their wounds, then we would feel less uncomfortable and would readily encourage them to cry. Never say to
the bereaved 'don't cry', but rather 'let yourself cry as much
as you need to.' Such a simple sentence can make a world of
difference, the difference that goes from a shallow time
together to a fertile encounter where the bereaved feels
understood.

Pressurising the bereaved to show feeling

This is exactly the opposite mistake. We cannot force anyone
to cry or show anger. The pouring out of emotions follows a
rule that must be respected at all times: it is spontaneous and
voluntary. We don't have the right to invade the most private
'room' of the mourner – their heart – and force a catharsis
which in this case will not be healing, but rather harmful.
Tears cannot be prevented, but trying to make someone cry is
not helpful. The Bible exhorts us to 'weep with those who
weep', not to force them to weep! This mistake often stems
from the wrong idea that there is no real grief without tears.
While it is true that the total absence of tears may indicate an
inhibited grief, we cannot equate the 'efficiency' of the grief

process to the outpourings of crying or anger, for the reasons mentioned earlier.

3 Understanding

'Thank you for understanding me; I really appreciate your understanding how I feel, my thoughts, my fears. You cannot give me back my son, but your attitude makes me feel better,' said a desperate mother to the pastor who used to visit her at her home regularly after the death of her adolescent son.

The bereaved have a great need to feel understood. Understanding is different from support. So far we emphasised their need to experience the warmth from the loved ones and to show emotions as the basic steps towards accepting. But, in due time, they also need to talk. In spite of their wish to be alone, they are more ready to put their feelings and thoughts into words and so dialogue is now possible. The bereaved are willing to talk about the symptoms and feelings they are experiencing, the memories of the funeral or even all the facts that surrounded the death, the relationship with the loved one, their virtues and character, 'how good he was', fears about the future, concerns about specific matters like money, etc. Now they are able to think more rationally than during the first weeks when they were very confused and their expression was mainly emotional, not verbal; although some mourners want to talk right from the beginning. But they will be choosy who they talk to. Some will want those they can easily cry with – and some will want the opposite – they don't want to be overwhelmed by other people's emotions when they are struggling with their own. Always remember when you are supporting someone who has been bereaved that however upset you are, they are more upset. Don't expect them to help you with your grief – find someone else who is more removed from the situation.

They may even raise spiritual questions such as 'Why did God let this happen?' or 'How can a good God allow so much suffering?' Now they are able to reflect deeply on all that happened, they start elaborating arguments. This was Job's experience: after the initial stage of numbness – when everybody around kept silence – Job needed to complain and put his feelings into words. In chapter 3 of Job we find his first discourse – eventually followed by several others – which show the tremendous need this pious man had for self-expression, but also for understanding. It is here precisely where both his wife and his friends failed completely. They were not a help to him, but rather a nuisance. What did they do wrong? Simply they said too much and were unable to understand Job's feelings and thoughts. In this two-fold mistake lies the essence of a good helping approach at this stage. Two requisites

- Empathy: be aware and understand the mourner's condition
- Be a good listener

Empathy

While in the first need – support – we mentioned the importance of compassion or sympathy, that is 'suffering together with'; now we introduce a new concept, empathy. Literally meaning to 'suffer from within', it is the capacity to understand how the other one feels. It implies such a genuine interest in that person that we 'put ourselves under their skin.' It is summarised with this attitude: 'If I were in their place, how would I react, think or feel?' 'How would I like to be treated?'

> One lady, who had never met my dad, was crying down the phone with me. That really helped, that someone cared enough to cry for me.[34]

Let us consider again one of the many texts where Jesus displayed an amazing amount of empathy towards the bereaved. On this occasion it was the death of a child which motivated Jesus to intervene: 'Soon afterwards, Jesus went to a town called Nain ... As he approached the town gate, a dead person

---

[34] Sarah Peacock, Interview, 2003

was being carried out – the only son of his mother, and she was a widow. ...When the Lord saw her, his heart went out to her and he said, "Don't cry."' (Lk.7:11-13). We know the rest of the story: Jesus returned this teenager to life and his resurrection caused great awe and praise to God (see verse 16). The point we want to emphasise here is the reaction of Jesus as he realised the intense suffering of this desperate mother. The expression 'his heart went out to her' reflects the idea of empathy very well: Jesus put himself in the situation of the woman and he understood how she felt.

Some of you may ask: is empathy something inborn, a natural gift, or can you also learn it? The answer is both. Empathy is indeed something you are born with, but also you can stimulate it. A good way to develop empathy and, therefore, our capacity to understand the bereaved, is learning to listen attentively, 'passionately' as the Swiss doctor Paul Tournier said.

Be a good listener

If the bereaved needs to talk, someone needs to be a receptive listener. Listening is one of the best tools we have to help a person in grief. This is a time to listen sensitively, to listen not only with your ears, but with your eyes! Such listening is a powerful instrument to show our genuine interest in the mourner. As we already said about silence, through listening we communicate messages – love, warmth, identification – which need no words because they are able to reach the heart directly. As a matter of fact, a true dialogue can happen when someone speaks and another one listens because there is communication from both sides; only one uses words, but the other one responds with attitudes and gestures which are eloquent enough.

I remember a woman who once came to see me to share about a difficult situation she was going through. She was talking without interruption for a whole hour; when I said we should stop and continue at another time, she quickly replied: 'Thank you, doctor, it was a very helpful conversation.' (!) I had not spoken a single word, but it was a conversation to her.

This case illustrates the importance of listening, listening a lot, without hurry, with great interest, with a loving heart. If you are able to do it, you have gone more than half way to help the person in need.

Why is listening so essential in grief? Listening makes us more specifically human. In what sense? The human being is the only animal in the creation that is able to listen. The other animals are only able to hear. This is so because listening requires that capacity for reflection that we call consciousness – the conscious thought – and this attribute belongs to human beings alone. If this capacity to listen is the ingredient which makes human communication unique, then we must promote it in bereavement, a time when human relationships are of vital importance.

The danger here comes from talking too much. Actually the Bible is full of references to this mistake and its dramatic consequences. The book of Proverbs warns us that 'When words are many, sin is not absent, but he who holds his tongue is wise' (Prov. 10:19). James is very keen in his letter to emphasise the terrible dangers of a wrong use of the tongue in our personal relationships. His summary is very relevant to our purpose in a grief situation: 'My dear brothers, take note of this: Everyone should be quick to listen, [and] slow to speak ...' (Jas. 1:19).

As we noted already in the earlier stages of grief, we are called to listen, not to preach. Nevertheless, if you are successful in showing adequate empathy and sensitivity, the mourner will probably tell you: 'Thank you for understanding me.' In this case, the door is open for some deeper talking and sharing. If you feel it is time for you to speak, be very honest, do not mask your feelings and do not try to prove or demonstrate anything. Your words should always be gentle, carefully measured, not overwhelming or aggressive. It is a time for sincere sharing, not for theological discussion. I remember a widow who was visited by a member of her church during her bereavement. Their 'fellowship' ended with a bitter theological dispute about the state of the soul in the 'intermediate state', that is the time between our death and the second coming of our Lord. The memory she kept of such a visit was not very encouraging: 'instead of comfort, she gave me a headache,' she complained to her pastor!

This is a time also for a wise use of the Scriptures, specially those texts which are encouraging and give hope. An appropriate use of the Bible is, no doubt, the best thing you can give to the afflicted by death. The word of God is 'living and active' (Heb. 4:12), powerful to provide Jesus' rest for those 'burdened and heavy laden' (see Mt. 11:28). Many of the Psalms are appropriate here, as well as those portions of the Gospels that show how Jesus identified with human suffering. Also if the bereaved raises concrete questions or topics, you can discuss them, even your own experience with death. A traumatic life event usually opens the door for deeper spiritual experiences, including getting to know God in a personal way.

4 Reorganisation

This fourth need correlates with the last stage of grief: adaptation. It is a time when the mourner is able to invest again their emotional energy – or at least part of it – in the everyday life with its duties, demands and concerns. As we already explained, it is a time of recovery and resolution which leads the bereaved to adapt to the new life without the meaningful loved one. The process can be long, complex and difficult depending on the several factors mentioned earlier.

How can we help here? The following suggestions are intended to accomplish the *adaptation* which is the ultimate step in the process. We are talking about the last stage; this means that most of these suggestions cannot be applied in the earlier phases of grief. Once more it is necessary to be sensitive to the grieving person's situation: we should start where they really are, not where we think they should be. Chapter 1 gives a checklist of indicators to show whether the bereaved has reached this stage.

- Encourage the grieving person to return to everyday life activities. Setting practical tasks and small goals for the day will help. Help them take decisions. When they are able to fulfil these small duties, a sense of victory will follow which, in turn, will stimulate their capacity to go on struggling. The first steps are always the most difficult ones.

- Challenge the mourner's idea that life is empty and meaningless. Help them recover the sense of the future by planning specific activities, appointments, outings, holidays, church meetings etc.

- Help them control their negative thoughts. The power of positive thinking is not only a modern assumption of some psychologists, but truly biblical advice summarised by Paul in one of his wise exhortations: 'take captive every thought to make it obedient to Christ' (2 Cor. 10:5b). Thoughts are like seeds that eventually will bring forth feelings and decisions. Remember, therefore, that if you want to change your emotions, you need to start with your thoughts.

- Encourage the bereaved to seek and participate in activities which may bring positive emotions to them; joy, gladness, pleasure. Remind them that pleasurable situations are God's will for our life: 'God ... provides us with everything for our enjoyment' (1Tim. 6:17). You should not feel guilty about this joy because the loved one who is missing would approve your being joyful rather than down and isolated. Withdrawal is not the best way to 'honour' the memory of the deceased.

- Help them achieve a satisfactory degree of *acceptance*. Accepting the death of a dear person is a long process and, in one way, never ends. Full acceptance in the sense that the missing one is forgotten is an impossible task. But a high degree of acceptance is possible, especially for Christians who have learnt 'the secret of being content in any and every situation' (Phil. 4:12). When Paul wrote this text he was in prison with many deprivations and had experienced a number of significant losses. His secret was in the uplifting grace of Christ '[which] is sufficient for [me]' (2 Cor.12:9). If we remember that to be able to accept the death of a loved one requires some satisfactory explanation – even if it is a partial one – of the loss, then we understand the central role of faith in such a process.

What helped us through – probably the most fundamental thing – was our relationship with God and our faith. I look back and I see my faith being tested in ways that it had never been tested before, or since, probably. And rather than shaking my faith, it did strengthen it...[36]

The Church as a therapeutic community

How can a local church help the bereaved? So far we have considered the help coming from individuals. What can be done from a group viewpoint? Even non-Christian researchers have recognised the relevant role that Christian communities can play in the grief process. The reason lies in the very nature of the church: it is a body where all the members are interconnected in such a way that 'If one part suffers, every part suffers with it' (1 Cor. 12:26). This natural solidarity – 'we are all members of one body' (Eph. 4:25) – is nurtured by the supernatural love that is not ours, but comes from God 'because God has poured out his love into our hearts by the Holy Spirit' (Rom. 5:5). This love of Christ 'compels us' (2 Cor. 5:14) to comfort those who are suffering and grieving. In this sense the church becomes a therapeutic community.

By its very nature, we could say that loving and supporting the bereaved is one of the tasks for which the church is well equipped. Helping the weak is at the very core of the teaching to the people of Israel in the Old Testament. In the book of Deuteronomy we find nine verses referring to the duty to care for the orphans and widows. This emphasis continues later on in the ministry of the early church: '[a religion] pure and faultless is this: to look after orphans and widows and their distress' (Jas.1:27). James had in mind exactly the two groups of people whose experience of bereavement is one of the most intense: the children who lose parents and conjugal grief. This has been God's concern for many centuries.

This therapeutic dimension is one of the values that the church is able to offer to our society today. In a world where

---

[35] Ali Risbridger, Interview, 2000

the family is in crisis, not being a secure shelter any more, a local church becomes a second family because it is indeed a family of families. God's promise in Psalm 68:6 is one of the verses that impressed me most when I started my work as a psychiatrist: 'God gives the desolate a home to dwell in (RSV) ['sets the lonely in families', NIV]. Whatever the reason for their desolation may be, the best blessing God has to give them is a family. What a challenge to us today when thousands of people suffer the deprivation of this basic gift: a family. I know at least six people who became committed Christians as a result of the warm support they received from local churches during times of grief.

The support to the bereaved is not a task limited to a few trained people within the church. While it is true that the pastor or elders are called to a special responsibility in this area, it is a mistake to believe that only a handful of specialised people are called to the pastoral care within the church. Paul's command to us is very clear: 'Carry each other's burdens' (Gal. 6:2). It is the privilege and the duty of every member of the body to care for their brothers and sisters. Which means that I can and must do something for my brother who is suffering. There is certainly a place for specialised counselling, as we see in the complicated forms of bereavement, but we should not neglect the biblical principle of the universal priesthood of all believers.

In which ways can the church help? Most of the forms mentioned so far can be performed by the church too: attending the funeral service, visiting the home of the deceased, being available for practical help and so on. But I would like to focus your attention on two ways of caring which are specific to the church and convey a powerful sense of support.

- Prayer
- Encouragement

There is another instrument the church has to build up the bereaved: the word of God, but it is so magnificent that it will require a whole chapter for itself.

Prayer

The prayers of intercession for the bereaved are an invaluable source of comfort. Either private prayers by the members of the church or in public at the prayer meeting, they are a deep expression of love and compassion. Paul expressed this idea clearly when he wrote to the Corinthians: 'we know that just as you share in our sufferings, so also you share in our comfort ... We were under great pressure, far beyond our ability to endure, so that we despaired even of life. Indeed in our hearts we felt the sentence of death' (2 Cor. 1:7-9a). And then Paul continues to mention the value of their prayers in such a difficult situation: 'On him we have set our hope that he will continue to deliver us, as you help us by your prayers' (vv 10,11).

It is not only the psychological benefit that 'someone remembers me', but specially the spiritual power that prayer contains. We firmly believe that prayers can change things, but they can also change people. This phenomenon has been thoroughly researched in the medical field in the last years with surprising results; several surveys show that those patients, for example after surgery or cancer treatment, who either prayed themselves or knew that others were praying for them, recovered better and more quickly than those who were not supported by prayer. The same is true for the grief process.

Prayer, however, loses most of it impact when it is used as a routine or in a superficial way. It should be done at the right moment – our words should always be seasonable – not as an automatic cliché which can be a devaluation of a precious tool. Be careful not to promise too easily 'I will pray for you' if you are not really committed to doing it. It can be a subtle way of taking the name of God in vain.

Prayer can be done not only for the bereaved, but also together with them. The role of the minister is especially relevant here: his prayers with and for the grieving person are deeply appreciated. Many of the individuals I prayed with in times of distress remember vividly these brief moments of spiritual intimacy, even many years later. This is the kind of sermon people never forget! 'Your short words were a great comfort to me; I will never forget that moment.' Obviously our prayers with the bereaved should be short and uplifting. It is not a time for 'long repetitions' or theological digressions.

Encouragement

What do we mean by encouragement? Why is this a specific task for the church? The word encouragement in the New Testament – in Greek *parakaleo* – is an extremely rich concept. Literally meaning 'to call alongside', it conveys the idea of counselling, comforting, encouraging, strengthening and caring, among a variety of meanings. It corresponds exactly with the ministry of the Holy Spirit in the believer because he is the *Parakletos*, the counsellor or encourager *par excellence*. It is also the word Jesus used in the second beatitude referring precisely to those who mourn. The wonderful promise is: 'Blessed are those who mourn, for they will be comforted (encouraged)' (Mt.5:4). It is a wholehearted attitude which implies identification with, sympathy; and whose result is basically the encouragement of others, especially those in distress.

The ministry of encouragement was one of the cardinal activities of the Apostolic Church. We find many texts which show the importance that Paul and the other church leaders gave to it. Barnabas, whose name means son of encouragement, was one of the most outstanding examples. There was also Tychicus, whom Paul sent to the Colossians 'that he may *encourage* your hearts' (Col. 4:8). Paul says of Philemon: 'Your love has given me great joy and *encouragement*, because you, brother, have refreshed (literally 'comforted') the hearts of the saints'. The apostle himself and Silas, 'After [they] came out of the prison, they went to Lydia's house, where they met the brothers and *encouraged* them' (Acts 16:40 – all authors' emphasis).

In which ways can the church encourage the bereaved in this New Testament sense? I will just outline a few examples, but every minister and church should develop creative ways to implement this vital ministry in accordance with their own culture and local features.

- *Pastoral visits*. To visit the bereaved is the first elementary way to support them. Some time for talking, listening, praying, reading a short word of the Scripture or just weeping together is one of the gifts the mourner will appreciate most. Apart from the church members, here again the presence of the pastor has no substitutes. At times of great distress, the minister is perceived as a protective figure, a kind of a father or – using the proper biblical metaphor – as the shepherd that cares for the sheep. His rod and his staff will certainly comfort the bereaved.

  We cannot emphasise enough the importance of these pastoral visits. I recommend pastors a certain discipline in this ministry by following a regular pattern: in the first month of the grief process, visit the bereaved every week if possible. After the first month and during the first year, once every four to six weeks. In the words of Thomas Murphy, an outstanding Presbyterian pastor from the nineteenth century: 'The afflicted ought to be carefully attended by the pastor even if it has to be done at considerable sacrifice of time and toil … Even if we must work harder before or afterward, we should find time to see them often.'[37]

- *Small home groups*. This is one of the places where you can support the bereaved better and allows a regular follow up of their emotional and spiritual condition. Such small groups in homes, either for Bible study or prayer, provide an environment of shelter and fellowship – another privilege of the Christian body – which results in personal growth and, above all, 'the growth in the grace and knowledge of our Lord Jesus Christ' (2 Pet. 3:18). As we shall consider in the last chapter, this is, after all, the ultimate goal for Christians in any experience, including grief, to 'become mature, attaining to the whole measure of the fullness of Christ' (Eph. 4:13). The participation in such groups should not start too early in the grief process. At least one month, preferably two, should pass by before inviting them to it,

---

[36] Thomas Murphy, *Pastoral Theology, The pastor in the various duties of his office* (New Jersey, USA: Old Paths Publications, 1996), 248

unless the bereaved themselves take the initiative. If the bereaved are already part of a home group, they should not stop attending it – unless they so wish for a time – because the warmth and support of the group is now more necessary than ever before.

- *Support groups.* The members of these groups are those who have gone through similar kinds of bereavement. A common cause for grief is their link. Actually, the more specific the link – that is, the cause of death – the better. It is a well-known fact that a great deal of help comes from those who previously experienced, firsthand, a similar loss; for example, parents who have lost children, or those who have lost life partners, or those who are going through the pain of divorce. These groups are aimed at sharing feelings, reactions, problems and providing mutual understanding. Because it may be difficult to find enough people from the same church to form one of these groups, they can be open to other Christian communities in the area, which gives an excellent framework for fellowship and new relationships. There are many support groups in the UK that are not faith-based, but can be very helpful.

- *Hospitality.* Invite the bereaved to your home for a meal or just to share some time together. Opening the doors of your house to the suffering person is one of the most biblical ways to express compassion. Amazing opportunities for deep conversation usually occur during a meal. According to the apostle Paul, there is a close connection between '[sharing] with God's people who are in need' (which obviously include those afflicted by grief) and the practice of hospitality (Rom. 12:13). But don't imagine that you are offering them a holiday from their bereavement and be guided by them in terms of conversation – and if they want to talk about their loss, let them talk.

- *Material needs.* As a church, be aware of the financial difficulties the bereaved can go through and meet them as much as possible. Think specially of young widows, even more if they have children. The early church in Jerusalem was very sensitive to this, as we see from the problem mentioned in

Acts 6:1: 'In those days … the Grecian Jews among them complained against those of the Aramaic speaking community because their widows were being overlooked in the daily distribution of food.' It is clear that the church leaders had some kind of organised work to attend the material needs of the weak properly, in this case the widows. What an example to us today! Offers to do the ironing, provide meals, do the shopping, the gardening, all the mundane tasks that still need to be done despite the grief … all these can be enormously helpful.

- Sometimes children will need minding while the mother is not at home. Or perhaps you can provide legal or accounting help, over matters which involve the house or the bank. All these offers of help from loving brothers and sisters in the church can relieve the pressures on the bereaved enormously. You cannot imagine the immense support it conveys. But specific offers of help, as we have already stated, are what is needed.

- *Outings.* Taking them with you for a short holiday or one day excursion can be very encouraging since it provides a lot of chances to express support and to talk. Or you could visit some place together that you know the bereaved is interested in. Think of practical ways to help.

How can helpers take care of themselves?

One question may come to the mind of our readers here: is there a right distance to keep so that I am not unduly affected by the suffering of the bereaved? How can I keep a balance between the needs of others and my own emotional health? This is an important issue which we cannot cover in due depth here. But some guidelines are necessary, because you cannot think so much of others that you neglect to take care of yourself. This was the bitter regret we read in the Song of Songs, '… [They] made me take care of the vineyards; but my own vineyard I have neglected' (1:6). Be careful not to make the same mistake; to neglect our own 'vineyard', the proper care of ourselves, is the main risk for a helper, specially in those situations – such as grief – where the direct contact with the reality of death is very draining emotionally.

Everyone in the caring professions knows about the danger of picking up other's people pain and about the difficulty of 'disconnecting' emotionally. It is actually the price you have to pay for being compassionate. Whenever you identify with those who suffer, some amount of pain and stress is unavoidable. Helping and caring, when done properly, imply giving out some of your emotional energy. This was the case of Jesus when he healed 'a woman … who had been subject to bleeding for twelve years' (Lk. 8:43). The Lord, despite the fact that the crowd around was pressing against him, noticed that someone had touched him. The reason? 'Someone touched me; I know that *power has gone out from me*' (Lk. 8:43-46 – authors' emphasis). For Jesus himself an act of healing implied giving out energy. We cannot compare, of course, his miraculous deeds with our caring attitudes. But the principle behind it is the same: curing and caring are always energy consuming. Hence the need to keep the right balance.

There are two dangers which should be avoided, especially relevant to those helping or counselling the bereaved.

Dependency. Too much contact may create a situation where the bereaved is emotionally relying on their helper. This happens often when the bereaved was previously a dependent person, especially if they depended on the deceased (remember the terms in which we defined this pathological relationship in chapter 2). If this is the case, the helper should carefully increase the emotional distance. This can be done in several ways, but I would like to mention one: do not say 'yes' to all the demands of the mourner, especially in terms of time. You can tell if a person is abnormally dependent when – regardless your efforts – they never seem to have enough, they need more and more. This insatiability is a key feature in identifying a potential risk in the helping relationship.

I remember the case of a couple who were doing a marvellous job in helping their sister-in-law, a young widow whose husband died of cancer. But they were caught up in a situation where all the free time they had as a couple was invested in her. She could not do without them – the main criterion for a dependent relationship – so she was clinging to them in all their outings. The situation affected their marriage relationship, which so far had been excellent. As marital tensions grew, they came to me for help. They were not aware of the cause of their problem and they showed great perplexity and concern since they had got along well for many years. As they discovered the root of the problem – the dependency of their sister-in-law had broken the dynamics of their relationship – they decided to diminish the time they would spend with her. A few weeks later, the result was a total recovery of the healthy condition of their relationship.

Burn-out. This may easily be the result of the previous problem. When all your free time is invested in others, you are very likely to neglect the biblical advice of taking care of yourself, as Paul reminded Timothy (1Tim. 4:16). Helping a person in distress, specially the bereaved, is emotionally draining. Inner renewal of your emotional strength is a must. If you overlook it, little by little you will run out of energy and become exhausted. Then you will have nothing to give and will be vulnerable to depression or a stress-related illness.

Also in this area Jesus gave us a perfect model with his attitudes towards rest after work. His intense caring ministry often made him so tired that he felt the need to withdraw alone to a quiet place to rest and to be in fellowship with the Father (see, for example, Mk.1:35 or Mt. 14:22,23). Physical, emotional and spiritual renewal were a constant feature of his ministry because his intense healing and comforting activity required this.

To put into practice all these suggestions requires love and time. These are the main requisites to help a person in a grief situation. It may be draining, it may seem fruitless, but all the efforts we make are worthwhile. We cannot imagine the good we do to a grieving person by giving them our love and a little of our time. Perhaps they will not express their gratitude until the dark pathway of bereavement is over. Even if they never say thank you for all your care, remember that '[we] should not become weary in doing good, for at the proper time we will reap a harvest if we do not give up' (Gal. 6:9). Our ultimate motivation is not the grieving person, but Jesus.

'If anyone gives a cup of cold water to one of these little ones because he is my disciple, ... he will certainly not lose his reward' (Mt. 10:42).

'Whatever you do, work at it with all your heart, as working for the Lord, not for men, since you know you will receive an inheritance from the Lord as a reward. It is the Lord Christ you are serving' (Col. 3:23,24).

4

When the loss is very painful:

helping in special situations

Losing a child is the worst thing that can happen to you.[37]

How can we help ourselves or others when bereavement is particularly painful? The short answer is – sometimes we can't and professional help is needed. This does not, of course, mean we can wash our hands of the bereaved and simply abandon them to the professionals, but it does mean being aware of what we can and cannot do. Grieving situations that are the most difficult include losing a child, losing a partner through divorce, which we will consider in the next chapter, and children grieving.

Grieving parents: counselling when children die

'The death of a child is forever,' said an expert on this kind of grief, referring to its long-lasting effects. Indeed, at any age the loss of a child is exceedingly hard to experience and to assimilate. No doubt it is the most intense loss a human being can ever experience. 'We are not aware of the fact that our children do not have a life guarantee. Their death utterly collapses the

---

[37] Sue Sutton, Interview, 2000

sense of our life. Hence the great pain and disruption their death brings forth.'[38]

Of the many stories of loss that we find in the Bible, the one of Jacob mourning for his beloved son Joseph is a paradigm of the terrible distress of this kind of loss. Joseph's supposed death when he was a teenager shatters the father and cripples him emotionally. He will never be the same person again in the future. His words are a good summary of the elements contained in this special grief.

> 'It is my son's robe! Some ferocious animal has devoured him. Joseph has surely been torn to pieces.' Then Jacob tore his clothes, put on sackcloth and mourned for his son many days. All his sons and daughters came to comfort him, but he refused to be comforted. 'No,' he said, 'in mourning will I go down to the grave to my son.' So his father wept for him' (Gen. 37:33-35).

Jacob was devastated by the unexpected loss of the one son despite the fact that he was surrounded by his eleven other sons, his daughters and the rest of the family. As we see from the text later on, he was unable to accept it and to adapt to life without Joseph. It is only when Jacob is convinced that his son is still alive that his strength is totally renewed and he goes through a kind of personal transformation which allows him to live seventeen more years in spite of his old age.

In previous chapters we have pointed out several distinctive aspects of the grief process when a child dies. Now we will focus our attention both on the reasons why this event is so traumatic and on the consequences for the parents. Again we will be pointing out some mistakes or dangers, with suggestions of help. It is a surprising fact that often after the death of a child, parents do not receive the same degree of emotional support and help as a widow who loses her husband. Perhaps this tendency to ignore their enormous need stems from some wrong conclusions which we would like to expose

---

[38] Quoted by Ramón Bayés, an outstanding Spanish expert on this subject.

here; we wrongly believe that they are strong enough to cope because they are young; or 'they will help each other; after all they are not alone, it is two of them together.' Grieving parents have great need of help and counselling and are one of the most vulnerable group of people in our churches. The pastoral care and the church community support is crucially important to prevent a subsequent crisis.

Here are some of *the reasons* why this type of loss is particularly difficult to bear:

- The deceased child is never forgotten. The memories and the thoughts of the missing child continue for many years, usually for the rest of the parents' lives. Although the dividing lines between normal and pathological grief are difficult to draw, very often the loss of a child can be included in the former group because of this chronic course. I remember a mother who lost an son at the age of ten after leukaemia; as the years passed by she followed children the same age as her son and imagined what he would have been like had he lived. She could not stop her fantasies and probably didn't want to. In one way or another, the children will continue to be present in their parents' hearts.

- The unique parent-child attachment. In a child's death, parents experience the loss of a unique relationship. This is so because children are almost an extension of their parents. Genetically, psychologically and socially they represent a prolongation of their parents' identity. The loss of a child means the loss of a unique part of the parents' identity: 'It is as if a part of myself had died.' One father said once after losing his child in an accident: 'The death of a child is what resembles most your own death.'

- The intense guilt feelings: father or mother are likely to feel responsible for the loss. Because they feel responsible for the child in life, they also feel responsible for the death. These feelings can happen at conscious and unconscious levels and contribute to the devaluation of the self which is typical of a depressive state: 'I am a disaster, I was unable to foresee or to stop the death.' This guilt often becomes irrational and obsessive, requiring treatment by a psychiatrist or psychologist.

The consequences

Grief for a child is like a mined pathway which may have destructive effects. A real blow up can happen within the family as a result of the loss. Be alert to these dangers! They can eventually destroy other lives too. The understanding of these reactions will guide the helper in assisting them in this process. Remember that any crisis can be two-fold: it contains dangers, but it also brings forth opportunities for growth and renewal.

I will mention the three most pervasive dangers which require adequate treatment. It's especially important to try to prevent them before they occur.

- *A crisis in the parents' marriage*
Many couples' relationships founder under the stress of the grief. According to several studies, an incredibly high number, such as 80 per cent, have significant marital tensions and up to 45 per cent end in divorce. The guilt feelings usually turn into accusations and reproaches, bitterness invades every corner of the relationship and communication becomes difficult. Suggestions for help here would include:

- Encouraging the spouses to talk to each other openly about their own feelings, but also about their partner's feelings. They must continue to do this for a long time, even years. A sensitive moment to do it is at anniversaries, when the sorrow is activated again by the memory.
- Encouraging the husband to express his feelings frankly, especially before his wife. It is not unusual for women to believe that their husbands are not as affected as they are because they do not react in the same way. Many men in our Western countries still believe that weeping is a sign of weakness and a lack of manhood. The man wrongly believes

that 'I must be the strong one in this situation. If she sees me weeping she will think I am failing.' Far from this, when the spouses cry together, they are investing in their own healing and in the strengthening of the marriage pillars.

- Sometimes, as is shown by the interview with Peter Reynolds, the man may grieve more openly than the wife – this is also completely normal.

- Encourage both of them to talk as much as necessary to the doctors who treated the child. It is important for them to hear that everything humanly possible was done and that there was nothing else that could have been done for the child. Anything to diminish guilt is welcome.

- Do not stop them if they want to talk about their child. They need to do this with friends or relatives, or with the surviving children. It is a natural way to assimilate the death and to relieve their pain.

- Encourage them to participate in one of the support groups we mentioned, where parents in similar situations share their experiences.

- Help them become aware that this traumatic crisis can be a unique opportunity to deepen the marriage. If the spouses are able to strengthen their mutual support and care as a result of the grief, their marriage will be extremely firm in the future. What an exemplary reaction David had after his infant son died. According to the text, the very first thing he did was to comfort his wife Bathsheba (see 2 Sam.12: 24). David cared for and deeply loved his wife while she was in the greatest distress a mother can ever have.

- *Parental inability to relate to the other children*
When a child in the family dies, the parents are not fully able to love and care deeply for the rest of the children for a time. Their grief for the deceased child is so draining that it seriously jeopardises their capacity to continue to be a healthy emotional support to the surviving children. In the next section we will look at the subject in more depth, but let us give some basic suggestions for help here.

- Devote a specific time of the day and the week to be with and play/talk/share with the other children. Father and mother must be emotionally available and the best way to do this is by setting a regular time, which will greatly help when they do not feel like being with them. Remember that 20 or 30 minutes every day is better than two hours every two weeks.

- Reassure them with words of hope and security. Parents who have lost a child should not forget that their children likewise have lost a brother or sister; they are struggling with their own grief too, from a much more vulnerable position. The parents' attitudes and behaviour hold the key to relieving their children's anxiety and pain.

- Do not hide your emotions or thoughts before your children, but be careful to balance them with positive feelings and attitudes. Remember there is a time for everything, a time to weep and a time for joy. This balance is critically important for a healthy emotional upbringing. It is not bad if your children see you weeping; the problem comes when they see you *always weeping*.

- *Parental health problems*

One of the features of parents' grief is the continuing distress despite the passage of time. They suffer a prolonged and intense distress which can eventually damage their health, either mentally or physically. It is striking that around 75 per cent report mental health problems. According to several surveys, mothers were more affected than fathers: they showed more intense reactions to the loss and poorer adjustment than the men. An interesting point refers to the bereavement emotional response in time, suggesting it diminishes in the second year and becomes more intense again in the third year.

The same principle applies to their physical health. The rate of disease, either somatic or psychosomatic, is dramatically raised in bereaved parents, and as we mentioned earlier, their expectancy of life is diminished too, most of the time because of such health problems. Our help here is quite obvious: we should encourage parents to overcome their likely indifference towards life and be good stewards of their health; for example, gently pushing them to arrange regular check-up visits with their doctor.

● *Wanting a new baby as a substitute*
Some parents are very keen to have another child. This is of course a totally legitimate decision provided that this later child does not serve as a replacement for the deceased. This wrong response to child loss is called the replacement child syndrome and reflects an incomplete mourning. Actually, some parents unconsciously believe that the new child will help to stop the grief process.

Parents who have lost a child may choose to have another child at any stage of the grief process. It is not a matter of timing – there is no rule regarding the right time to want a baby – but of having the right motivation. The purpose should never be to forget the lost child or to diminish the pain of the grief. The joy of another child should be compatible with the sorrow for the lost one. Again it is a matter of 'everything in its own time' and place. Actually a later child may help them to reorganise and adapt to the new situation. It may provide new goals and new relationships, all of which are highly desirable in the last stage of grief.

Counselling when children grieve

Children grieve too. What an obvious statement and yet how often we neglect it! Sometimes it is because the adults around are themselves grieving and they lack the emotional energy to pay attention to the little ones. Other times it is because we simply do not know what to tell them. Despite their good will, many adults feel unable to approach the younger members of a bereaved family. So, either nothing is said to them or some story full of fantasy is substituted for the truth. In both cases, silence or untruthful imagination, we are not helping the grieving children.

The normal difficulties many people have in relating to someone grieving are increased with children because most of us have completely forgotten how a child thinks and sees life. The world of children is totally different from that of adults. Therefore we cannot treat them as little adults, because they are not. To deal with the subject properly would require another book. For those who want to go deeper in this area of child bereavement I warmly recommend the book *Children and grieving*[39] by Dr Janet Goodall, a paediatrician whose wide experience in this realm underlies the very practical approach of her book.

Following the outline of Janet Goodall's book, for practical purposes we will separate children into four groups according to their age. The reason is obvious: we cannot generalise and include all children in one category. Children vary so much that the principles and suggestions for a six-year-old child cannot be applied to a ten-year-old. Their capacity to understand reality, including death, changes a lot according to their mental and emotional development, and also according to their own experience. These changes will determine both their reactions in the face of death and our approach to them. 'Tuning in to the right wave-length is vital if we are to help a grieving child.'[40] So we should know some basic points about these four groups which are:

- Infants and toddlers
- Three to seven year olds
- Eight to eleven year olds
- Adolescents

In the case of adolescents their grief pattern is very similar to that of adults. For this reason we will not consider it separately here. The most significant point at this age is the risk of behaviour problems and substance abuse. Both of them can be an expression of their bereavement, as pointed out in chapter 2. Depression may be the final outcome and then proper treatment is very helpful.

---

[39] Janet Goodall, *Children and Grieving*, (Milton Keynes: Scripture Union, England, 1999)

[40] Janet Goodall, *Children and Grieving*

● *Infants and toddlers: children up to about two years old*
The first need is to recognise that babies can feel bereaved and
to identify this condition. A baby experiences distress in the
same way that they are able to experience love. Mothers are
very good in interpreting correctly the crying of the baby and
the kind of need that is to be met. Some people wrongly
believe that 'a child is not at all aware of what is happening,'
as if they were sleeping objects! This is a mistake. The child is
not absent, far away from the emotional environment, because
he or she is a real person from the beginning. This is why
babies experience the warmth of a close relationship, but also
experience the pain when such closeness is broken or missing.

The worst loss for a baby is to be separated from the person who was closest to them, usually the mother. A sudden
ending of such emotional link, regardless of the cause, is
experienced by the child as a rejection. When a child feels
rejected this leads to bereavement. Such grief is usually
expressed through crying, a special kind of crying, different
from other times, that the expert mother or caretaker should
pay attention to and be able to identify. The recovery from
such loss is achieved through the presence of some other
familiar person who may gradually restore the deep attachment which is a source of security and warmth. The goal here
is to recognise and meet the needs of the child, specially the
emotional ones: closeness and warmth. The physical expression of love will be very helpful. It may take days or weeks,
but time will bring healing much more quickly than in the
older children.

If possible the child should not be sent away to stay with
someone who is totally new to them. A new family setting
adds new stress to the child, who is already struggling to
adapt to a new situation. Their normal routine should be kept
up as much as it can be. The guiding rule here would be 'make
as few changes as possible.'

● *Children from three to seven years*
This age is probably the most difficult in terms of grief orien-
tation. For these children reality and fantasy are difficult to

separate. They have an incredible imagination. Their thinking is almost magic and any description needs to be matched by experience. These are the main guidelines for helping them:

- Prepare the child as much as possible. Some sensitive and gradual preparation for the actual death is ideal because the outcome of the grief is strongly linked to its expectancy. The more unexpected the death, the more complicated the grief (as we saw with adults). Of course, sometimes it is not possible. Sudden deaths give no chance of this. But a long disease, cancer for example, when death approaches slowly, gives plenty of opportunity to face and assimilate the reality. When children are carefully prepared, the prognosis of the grief is far better than in the cases when this preparation is lacking. This principle applies to children at all ages. How can we prepare the child? This leads us to the next suggestion.
- Tell the truth little by little. Do not say too much too soon. The wise principle of the progressive revelation, which God used with us in the Bible, should be applied here. Truth can be told in stages and for children at this age this is the best method. A common mistake is to give too much information to the child, information which they haven't asked for and which is not relevant to their needs. This can bring more confusion than help.
- A practical way to do it is by giving the child some short pieces of information and then wait for their questions. These questions reflect the real problems, doubts or interests of the child in such a way that answering them is much more relevant than your own ideas. It is better to say too little and wait for questions than too much and create unnecessary problems. Let the curiosity of the child be your guide.
- Call death by its name. Do not avoid it. Using other names, usually euphemisms, can be very confusing. Dr Goodall mentions the case of a child who was told that her dead brother had gone to sleep. No wonder she had insomnia for weeks. She was afraid to go to sleep because her brother had not returned from this state. Also the word 'loss' should be avoided since it can mean that some day 'the lost

may be found.' Although their understanding of death varies with their age, specially its implications, most if not all children are familiar with death itself. They have seen it in nature, for example with flowers or insects. We, as adults, have many more problems than children in referring to death openly.

- Give children the option to see the dead body. Seeing a dead body will make less impression on a child this age than it will on the adults. Part of this is because many children believe that death is still reversible. It can be understood as a natural way to say goodbye. It is not until a later age that children are fully aware of the meaning and implications of death. As a matter of fact this is a wonderful protection God has given children, but death remains a delicate situation for them, and it should be prepared for and handled with sensitivity. You should give them the freedom to see the body or not. If you notice that they hesitate or feel reluctant, do not try to persuade them. It is a mistake to pressurise them against their will. Usually older children prefer to avoid this and their wishes should be strictly respected.

- Attending the funeral. There is a lot of discussion about whether it is good for children at this age to participate in the funeral or not. From about three years old upwards, children are more able to understand the meaning of this kind of service, yet the objection comes from the emotional atmosphere which may surround it: seeing mother or father, brothers or sisters in deep pain, crying a lot and sometimes literally despairing, does not seem a very appropriate place for a little child to be. My feeling is that it is good to include the child in the family plan even when it is a sad one, rather than risk them feeling rejected. But if you foresee that the funeral will be a time of a lot of emotional expression, when pain and even desperation will be higher than solemnity, then you should be cautious in taking the child. We do not want the children to be hurt by another traumatic experience. They have enough coping with the loss itself.

- Grief overlooked and adult depression. Children who suffered an important loss before the age of seven or eight, especially of their father or mother, report a high percentage of chronic depression when they are adults. This traumatic life event shapes their personality in such a way that they are prone to inferiority feelings, they show a great need to feel loved, hypersensitivity and other signs of emotional deprivation. No doubt the reason is that their needs during the grief period were not properly met. Neglecting the care of the tender wounds of the child will eventually turn these wounds into complicated scars. They felt lonely and unwanted. This is not unusual when the grown-ups are so absorbed in their own sorrow that they lack the energy to take care of the little ones. Beware of this common mistake: do not forget, children grieve too! Their future personality may greatly depend on how you care for them during this critical period.

- Feeling guilty about the death. Clarify as much as possible that they are not to blame for it. Children at this age have a great tendency to feel guilty and blame themselves for many things. It is quite possible for them to believe that the reason for the death of the loved one is their bad behaviour or their little quarrels at home with a brother or sister. Take all the time you may need to explain carefully that this is not so. Clarify that things which happen around them are not the result of their misbehaviour.

- Signs of grief at this age may not always be obvious, so the care-givers must be alert to any change in the previous personality or mood. It may include tears, but also more subtle signs such as altered behaviour. The child changes for the worse, feels irritable and argues over any small detail. It is not simply that he or she is now a naughty child – the reason behind it is deeper: the child's misbehaviour is expressing a lot of pain. This is their way of communicating their need for attention and affection.

  At other times, bereaved children may be very quiet, unnaturally so for a child, which is a mask covering the sorrow inside. Another possible change is regression, that is, babyishness: their behaviour goes back to earlier stages. An attitude that is particularly important, which also occurs when parents divorce, is an anxious clinging to someone, usually the surviving parent. This intense separation anxiety is shown in the child being afraid of being left alone, or being afraid of going to school, in case they lose the surviving parent.

In all these cases, the attitude of the care-givers should be one of understanding and tolerance. Patiently go along with these different behaviour patterns and they will diminish and eventually disappear. You should not be rigid or harsh because then you are worsening the child's feeling of rejection which is at the core of their bereavement.

How else can I help?

The grieving child has two great needs which we will define in negative terms: they should not feel lonely and they should not feel unwanted or rejected. To prevent these two situations you can do several practical things, many of which we already mentioned earlier. We could summarise them in four steps:

- *Be aware* of their emotional needs in grief; remember children express such needs in a language which is different from the adult.
- *Talk to them* and tell what they need to be told – the right amount of information.
- *Do not exclude them* from the family environment; they need to feel included, that they are a part of the family.
- Be willing to *offer time* and emotional *strength* for careful listening.

- *Children from eight to eleven years*
Many of the comments made for the previous group can be applied here too, so we will not repeat them. There are, however, some specific items for this age that are worthwhile considering.

- Clarify fears. Children at this age already have a sense of anticipation and, as a result, they may show anxiety and fears about the future. A death in the family may raise the fear that something similar will happen to them or to some of their other loved ones. For example, they may expect to die at the same age as their brother or sister. Or they may show a lot of anxiety if any health problem reminds them of the symptoms that the dead relative had. Talking to them and clarifying all these fears will help. Unlike many adults who find it difficult to trust the information given to them, children are very responsive to words of reassurance; one short conversation can have long-lasting effects.

- Facilitate emotional expression. Children find it very difficult to put their feelings into words. They hardly ever talk about how they feel. Therefore it is important to provide other channels for them to let their grief out. A good one is through drawing. It is amazing to discover how much outpouring a child can achieve through painting, drawing or even inventing stories. Playing with them is also helpful as certain games are very good for self-expression. All these tools provide the helpers with good clues to know what is going on in the mind of the child and provide excellent opportunities to start a conversation. We can never emphasise enough the need that the grieving child has to talk over what is happening. Ignoring their grief by keeping silent is exactly what *you should not do* if you really want to comfort a child.

- Grief expressed by bodily symptoms. It is quite usual for children at this age to suffer from psychosomatic troubles as an expression of unresolved distress. Poor appetite, loss of weight, headaches, abdominal pains, bed-wetting and other symptoms may indicate that there is no satisfactory development of the grief. The persistence of these troubles should make parents alert to some emotional needs that are not being met. Unfortunately, some parents are not aware of the body-mind connection in children, so they neglect the emotional side of the problem in trying to find physical causes for the child's health problem. Then a vicious circle is started because the anxiety of the parents increases the distress of their child and the physical problem worsens.

- When is counselling necessary? There is one clear indication for professional advice, when the child has been present at someone's sudden or violent death. Post-traumatic stress disorder – explained earlier – affects children too and requires a specialised treatment. Especially distressing are the visual memories which may be so severe as to prevent normal life. Reassurance to the child and to the parents that improvement will follow – though it may take months – is usually very relieving.

We cannot close this section without remembering the memorable words of Jesus about children: 'Let the little children come to me, and do not hinder them, for the kingdom of God belongs to such as these' (Mk.10:14).

For this reason, our last suggestion for help has to do with the spiritual needs of the children.

- Provide words of hope. Above all, share with the grieving child the hope we have in Jesus. The person that we miss so much now is under the care of the loving Jesus who is in heaven. This is a good opportunity to explain what Heaven will be like, a place where there are no tears or sickness. Finally, tell them that one day we will meet again in heaven with our Lord Jesus. We will have a big, big celebration. Then we will be together for ever and we will not need to say goodbye any more. This is the wonder of the message of the gospel: it is at the same time so inscrutable that no one can fully grasp its depth, but also so simple that a child can understand its essence.

* * *

Peter and Barbie Reynolds were busy pastoring a church and running marriage workshops around the country when their 21-year-old son, Simon, died following a car crash in South Africa, in December 1993. Since then, they have set up the Bereaved Parents Network, part of Care for the Family, and they frequently talk to groups of bereaved parents.

Peter Reynolds

A phone call came through from South Africa to say that Simon had been involved in a road accident and was in a coma, was comatose, and the hospital said there was a 50/50 chance of his survival. A cold shudder went through me – I felt very, very cold – that's a classic sign of shock. I think it wasn't so much the fact that he had been in a road accident but that there was a 50/50 chance of his surviving that was unthinkable to me.

After Simon's death, when we were in South Africa, I just felt a deep, deep ache it was like walking in a dream. I was dazed, on auto-pilot, with this deep ache in the pit of my stomach. Partly it was because we were finally visiting South Africa – he had asked us many times, 'Please come out, it is so beautiful,' he wanted us to go, and there we were in the beautiful Cape, which he had thought was so fantastic and had longed for us to come and see – and he wasn't able to show us around. I felt desperate waves of regret that things had happened the way they had. He had written to us just a little while before, saying he knew he loved being in South Africa but he longed to come home for a cup of coffee with us, and there was deep regret that we didn't just find the money and say 'Come home!' If he had, then of course the accident would never have happened. Simon had a sum of money coming to him but the money hadn't yet been released. It was released – the actual money came through just a matter of a day or two before his accident so the other regret was that I wished I had been able to say, 'Hey Simon, there is this money coming out to you now' and that would have released him to get on a plane.

Did you ever doubt God?

I was so convinced of the goodness of God because of how kind he had been to me since I gave my life to Jesus Christ. So there was never any anger – if anything, I blamed myself. How much of this was my fault, because I was conscious that when I heard the news, I wasn't praying. Why on earth wasn't I close enough to God to know my son was struggling for his life? The time he actually had the accident, Barbie had just come back from the States and we were trying to catch up because she came back to the news that our youngest grandson had died. I blamed myself that I wasn't in tune enough in God to know … if anyone was at fault, it was me. It certainly wasn't God – he is such a good God.

Even ten years later I sometimes still think, oh God, take me home. The loss of Simon wasn't the only thing that I was having difficulty with at the time – it came at a difficult time. Was this me being exposed in some way, some attack on our family? But afterwards, for at least six months, I just didn't want to go on living. I would go for a walk in the fields all around and I would be crying out to God and be saying, please, please take me home, I don't know how to pull myself out of this one. There just didn't seem to be any way of getting out. It was like being in the bottom of a pit, like the Psalmist said, it was very muddy and slippery and I was trying to get out of this pit. I would try and get a foothold and my foot would slip – and I knew I just couldn't get out of this one. I was wiped out, finished, I didn't know how to recover and it was in that despair I was saying, God, please take me home, I don't want to go on living on this earth. And then it moved from there and I would be saying, God, if you aren't going to take me home, you're going to have to do a miracle inside me because I can't do this by myself. I couldn't pull myself up by my bootlaces and say, 'Come on, Peter, get going.' I had done that many times in the past but I couldn't do it this time, I was finished.

It was the combination of so many deaths in the family, it was a feeling of what on earth's happened? Have I lost it in God? Our twenty-one-year-old nephew was killed in a micro-lite accident; there was my mother; there were various uncles and aunts as well, and then of course Timothy, our grandson, just before Christmas, so it just felt like 'Are you so displeased with me or what is this?' I wasn't suicidal, I wanted God to do it. I wanted my life to be in God's hands but as I was wailing and crying and sobbing and walking in the woods and sometimes just having agonised shouts of pain from the depths of my tummy – the only thing that came through there was the Scripture where Paul says 'if the same Spirit that raised Christ from the dead was inside you' – in the old King James it says – 'then he will quicken life in your mortal body.' That Scripture would go round and round in my mind and 'if faith comes by hearing, hearing by the word of God' – some would say, that was what was happening and God was gradually building in me a cry that came out many, many times. 'God, unless your Holy Spirit inside me quickens life in me, then I'm a goner. Lord, you can do that and you'll have to do a miracle inside me.' The thing that comforted me, as I prayed, is that Paul was referring to Jesus and Jesus was dead, he was in the tomb, it wasn't Jesus' faith that did it, he was finished, he was dead. He wasn't in a swoon – it was the activity of God that did it, by the power of the Holy Spirit, so that would give me a little glimmer of hope: God, you did it for Jesus, it is over to you because I can't do it.

I knew Barbie would be grieving – perhaps I had inflicted this grief on her, because it was my fault, as head of the family, because I wasn't praying ... she was grieving but she hardly cried. I wasn't able to be a comfort to her – I didn't have any comfort to offer her. We have talked about this many times since with hundreds and hundreds of bereaved parents and we have gone through this story ... only one in four marriages survives the death of a child, they say. You can understand how couples fall apart.

I don't believe it was my fault now because I can see the sovereignty of God in it all and I can see that what happened has been part of a master-plan. I still have questions, and can I say God wanted it in the first place? I am not sure I can say that in terms of my own theology and my own understanding of the goodness of God but God certainly allowed it and I can see indications now so clearly that God knew it was going to happen, and there were certain things that happened way back that I could say to you which made me realise that was a supernatural moment: God saying you don't know what is coming but I want you to feel some things here, and it was so clear that God knew it was going to happen. It didn't take God by surprise. So now I don't beat myself up about it, because I know Simon is in a fantastic place. We considered, even when Simon was in the morgue ... I remember one night Barbie saying we could go right now and raise him from the dead, why not? And we prayed about that, and we knew that was not right, we would just be going through the motions

and that God was not going to do that ...was that lack of faith? But in
the end you can only do what you see your heavenly Father doing.
Jesus said the Son of Man can't do anything by himself ... we felt he
was in a place where he would much rather be, rather than be sum-
moned back to earth.

What did people do that helped?

Paul Wakely (the senior elder) covered so lovingly, made no
demands on us, there was never any sense of putting pressure on us.
We had hundreds of cards and letters and some people sent photos
of Simon that they had got tucked away and those things were fantastic. We had those cards up for weeks and weeks and we read them
and they were a great comfort to us, particularly from people who
weren't just saying they were sorry but who would tell stories about
Simon – things that he had done, things that he had said, things that
they had appreciated about him – all of those were tremendously
comforting to us, that his life had counted. Then Wesley Richards
read out the poem, that Simon had adapted on risk, at Spring Harvest
– three hundred young people responded to the call of God to give
themselves to serve God anywhere in the world and those things
were a great comfort.

There was one couple in Southport, the church group there, and
whether it was from them personally or the church I don't know, but
every year for the next five, six years they would send us a beautiful
flower arrangement on the anniversary of Simon's death or Simon's
glory day, as we call it. And this thing would come without fail, and
it was not just a flower arrangement, it was a magnificent one, until
we eventually saw them and said (we would thank them each time)
'Look, it is so fantastic but you don't have to do this for the rest of our
lives,' so they said, 'OK, that will be the last, then.' That was fantastic, over the top and wonderful.

Things that we now know would have been good (and we have
heard so many times from hundreds of bereaved parents) is that people wouldn't just avoid them... people wouldn't see them coming in
the supermarket and dash down another aisle, when they knew they
had seen them. We always say that bereaved parents are the most
awkward people because either people do the wrong thing by not

saying something or they do the wrong thing by what they say – we are just very, very awkward people. We loved people talking about Simon, we loved people looking at photographs … Barbie made a photographic album of Simon's life, the story of South Africa and she did it beautifully and wrote it all up and we loved people looking at that. The thing that was hard – one guy came and visited us, and it was lovely he came, he was one of the few people who came and sat with us, but we offered him the album and he wasn't interested and didn't look at it and he didn't have anything to say about Simon. So we thought it was lovely that he came but it would have been great if he had asked us questions about our loss.

People made us meals, that was fantastic, they either brought them round or had them delivered, and that was wonderful because we couldn't even begin to think of shopping. When we got back from the funeral, it was Christmas morning, all the Christmas decorations were up, and we had a Christmas meal that Frances Neale had cooked us – she tried to make it Christmas Paul Wakely rented a van and drove to Heathrow and picked us up on Christmas morning – what sacrifice for a family man that must have been, to leave his family early on Christmas morning, to drive through the snow to Heathrow, to bring us back to Bath.

People who said they wanted to do something for us, and would act on their own suggestions, that was great. You can't ask them because you can't even think what you need. People who would say 'I'd like to do this for you, is that OK' – you would say, 'Fantastic.' But if they would say 'Give us a call if there is anything we can do to help' – you never call them because you can't think of what you need anyway. You're hurting too much.

We talk about Simon because he is still our family and people will suddenly go very silent, shocked that we still talk about him … and we would even laugh about him, the way the milk bill had gone down since he had gone, and it was almost as though people were shocked that we could talk like that … and we would say we couldn't wait to be with him in heaven, there was going to be a great party in heaven … and you realised what you were doing was something that people couldn't cope with so we had to tone ourselves down sometimes for the sake of others. Is it a British cultural thing? I don't know the answer to that. Some societies do make a lot of mourning, and even if it is an external form, they have mourners and they go through all sorts of symbolic seasons of mourning ... even within the UK, our Asian friends will go and visit, whatever part of the country they are in, they will just go and visit. We have sat with Asians who have lost a wife ... just sat in their home. You don't have to say anything. But that is their style. We have got a strange way of handling death in our generation, though that does seem to be changing. It is ten years since Simon died and we do find it refreshing that more and more people do seem to be able to talk about loss.

We always say to people now, you have lost a part of you, you have lost a part of your family, and that loss can never be made up for. People say: 'You're still young, you can have other children' or 'At least you have got other children' or 'At least you have got each other – husband and wife.' The loss can never be made good again, you have lost that part of your family and that part of you has gone. To me, I felt like I had had a leg amputated and I was having to learn to walk without my other leg – I've got to learn to live again but I don't know how to do this because I have never been this way before.

I have had dreams galore over the last ten years, he is in the dream and I am flinging my arms around him; he was 6'7" and I had to stand on tiptoe – I want to see him, I want to hold him – those are constant or recurrent desires and longings ... I have loads of dreams ...

At first, the loss consumes everything and doesn't fit into your life, but after a period of time, it becomes part of your life but it fills it, and gradually your capacity to absorb it grows – but the loss is still the same, it hasn't diminished.

It is like a sharp jagged stone inside you, that keeps turning and cuts and cuts and cuts – and you feel the pain of it ... and it is just unbearable. Over time those jagged edges get worn down a bit, they are not so sharp, so the stone is still inside you and it still moves but it doesn't hurt so much. I don't know how people can cope without God, without knowing there is a supernatural God who is able to do what we can't do. That was the hope that came to me that meant I was able to get up and get going again. I am not surprised at all that people don't get over the loss of a child.

We got drawn into spending time with other bereaved parents because people would come to us and say 'My next door neighbour's son, who was twenty-one, their only son, has just been killed in an accident, and what do we do? What do we say?' so we would find ourselves counselling with others. We would read in the paper about a child being killed in a road accident, and Barbie would write a card saying 'our son was killed in a road accident and here is our telephone number if you would like to contact us' and every single time people would respond immediately with a phone call and we would find ourselves arriving on somebody's doorstep and the husband and the wife falling into our arms, complete strangers, sobbing and sobbing. And that happened in the Bath area and when we moved up here, so we realised there was a colossal need. So it is that sort of thinking that started the Bereaved Parents Network ...

It is harder for somebody to empathise if they haven't had a loss ... the number of times people say 'I went to my GP and they put me onto a counsellor for counselling and I went once but I felt angry with the counsellor because they were saying all the right things but they hadn't suffered the loss.' And yes, I wanted to talk to somebody who had suffered the loss, who had lost their son or daughter. I wanted to talk to somebody who had survived, somebody who knew God and loved God and had suffered the loss, because that reassured me that it wasn't just me, because of my own failure as a servant of God – those people were very hard to find.

The number of times I have said to groups of bereaved parents, including the fathers, that I didn't want to go on living – that statement – men all round the room start to surface, thinking 'but he's a bloke.' I say I cried every day for six months , I was supposed to be the man, my wife didn't cry; I was supposed to be the strong one, comforting her, but I was like a jelly, I lost it ...

What would you say to anyone who has just been bereaved?

Don't beat yourself up. The most fantastic thing that helped us again and again and again was a pastor in Sri Lanka, George Jacob, who wrote to us after the death of Simon, and I said to Barbie this particular letter I am looking forward to opening ... all he wrote was 'Be kind to yourselves.' And I thought – what does he mean? I don't know what he means ... be kind to yourselves. It didn't register but it was one of those things that was a living word and went round and round and round inside and we have said this to so many people: 'Be kind to yourself.' There will be so many things that flood through your mind, that it was your fault, or if only this had happened or if only this hadn't happened or why did it happen and all the rest of it – be kind to yourself because God isn't beating you up.

Barbie Reynolds

When I heard the news, I was shaky, I think I had a nose bleed … all the symptoms of shock. We had so much to do that day that I went into organising mother mode: I remember thinking 'This is bizarre. It is like packing to go on holiday because our son has just died.' It was like watching a movie; it was a weird feeling … it wasn't real … meeting Simon's friends, they moved out of the house [Simon had in South Africa] so we [the whole Reynolds family] could all move in: we didn't want to be separated from anybody in the family, we wanted to be together all the time.

I didn't cry then … there were certain times when I cried … I feel physical pain in my tummy … grief to me is pain in my tummy. I find it very easy to cry about other people and their pain but for myself and my family, I just feel pain in the pit of my stomach. It was too deep for tears. I remember when we came back from South Africa, and everybody was downstairs watching a movie, probably Boxing Day, and I thought, I will open Simon's suitcase and get his stuff out. When I opened it I just broke and I howled and howled and howled. I was so pleased that I was on my own – it was all right for me to cry if I was on my own – I was really glad that nobody was there and nobody was going to stop me … and I howled – everything I pulled out, I just howled. So I could cry, it wasn't that I can't cry, I wasn't bottling it up but I don't cry. Even when the feelings were the worst, I didn't cry … I just felt ill, I had pains in my stomach and chest pains; I just felt really ill. I knew they were all to do with grief, I knew they were stress related, so I didn't go to the doctor.

Peter was useless. I could see that he desperately needed to be comforted and I wanted him to comfort me but when he tried, it made it worse. If I started to cry, he would say 'What's the matter?' I'd say, 'What do you think is the matter?' It made me cross rather than comforted. It made me not want to cry when he was around because he would ask me what was the matter and that would make me cross. But I felt terrible for him, he was in so much pain, his whole face was haggard, he looked old and my greatest concern was, would he get through this? He was totally broken. I had never seen him like that before …he wasn't really there. You would find him weeping all the time. He would go out for his long walks, shout and holler … I would be driving along in the car and I would look across at him and he [would] have tears pouring down his cheeks and it was so sad. It was awful … he had given up inside. He couldn't cope with people and that was a great pressure. He was my greatest worry … he was the pastor, I felt he was supposed to be OK – supposed to be able to get through this.

It took a whole year before I went to a group for bereaved parents and then I only went because I was taking someone else … it was a whole year before I owned the term bereaved parents. I wasn't one of them … they were people who sat around moping. At Compassionate Friends I heard other people saying things that Peter said that I thought were really strange. We learnt there that everything we were going through was normal.

Peter wanted to know every single detail … to me, it felt like an obsession. So when we went to South Africa, he wanted to go out to the crash site and I didn't … but I didn't say anything. I am so glad I did now. We went to the first hospital Simon went to and Peter wanted to speak to the staff. I can remember it was a whole day of this, going to places, waiting to meet the staff, talking to them and going onto the next place – it was extremely important to Peter, every little detail, he wanted to talk to the ambulance drivers, and for three months after we got back to England he was trying to trace a witness in South Africa. He had to do it and he did it, but for me, it was 'Why do we have to know all that stuff?' So we had completely different reactions – but we now know that is completely normal – and they aren't gender specific.

Then he had this fear that we were going to forget Simon, which I thought was really peculiar. In his mind it was, ten years down the line, 'Oh yeah, we used to have a son called Simon … I remember him.' I was thinking 'Of course we won't' but it was very real to him. Now we know that is part of bereavement and that's why people won't let go, they won't move on, because they are afraid of forgetting

... so we do a whole thing of how you take the person with you. So it was only by going to a group and hearing a lot of other men talking that I realised my husband isn't so strange after all ... most bereaved parents have not been bereaved before, they have never lost a child before, they have never met anyone who has, so how do you know what is normal? But him reacting differently, it hindered me, we hindered each other. It needn't if you understand that but we didn't understand that. Our marriage survived by the grace of God.

I was never angry with God over Simon – he was the one person I could run to and I ran to him. We had a lot of people putting things on us ... they didn't say them to us, but to the kids ... and Peter says it was a good job they didn't say them to him, he probably would have punched them. They said there must have been sin in Simon's life, it must have been that Simon wasn't praying; because the church who sent him out weren't praying enough, because we his parents weren't praying enough – that there was something wrong with us and the covering over him was broken, and the enemy found a foothold. By implication there was some sin in our lives ... that this was Satan's doing. Some people thought Simon had a death wish and wanted to die and others that he shouldn't have gone to South Africa so he was out of the will of God and you are in the middle of it all, grieving and you're trying to work out does it matter anyway?

One of the things that hurt me most was somebody in leadership wrote a card, which said, 'Let us know if there is anything we can do to help.' This is the stupidest thing to say to a bereaved parent. It really hurt me much more than I would have expected because they were leaders and they should have known better and they didn't come and say it, they never spoke to us. I have to keep reminding myself that they did care, they just didn't know what to do.

God was my Rock and my Source. He held onto me the whole way through. What I longed to do was to talk to people who had been through it ... I don't think Jonathan and Sylvia Wallis realise how important they were to me ... Jill Stenning was fantastic, she would always come and sit with us on a Sunday ... Rose Ford used to cook for us, that was the only home-cooked food we would have in the week; we just lived on anything that would cook itself in the oven, oven chips, oven pizzas, whatever, that I didn't have to think about.

One couple invited us for Sunday lunch, and I had made this album, which was very important to us ... we used to laugh at ourselves – we would never leave it in the car in case the car got stolen... I can remember taking it with us when we got invited out to lunch, but they wouldn't let us show it – 'All that is in the past' – they wouldn't allow us to mention Simon. When your life is full of grief it is very hard to have trivial conversations or even important conversations about anything else so the kindest thing they could have done would have [been to] let us talk about Simon for the entire time. The lunch was great but it left us feeling frustrated and empty. They were trying, they thought 'We really want to bless Peter and Barbie, we will take them out of themselves and we are not going to dwell on all of that stuff.'

What would you say to newly-bereaved parents?

I would listen and reassure them that everything they told me I had heard before.

The thing I dread is being asked how long will it take? People want to be told in three months time, you'll be through this. Grief is a journey, coming to terms with your loss – and it is a very long journey and when you are starting off, you don't want to be told it is a horrendously long journey, you want to know it will be over quickly, by the end of next week, please. And then you read these books which tell you you're in stage one – the shock – and then there [is] stage two, stage three ... and I have heard parents say we're in stage four now, and you say 'Hmm...' in actual fact they are still in shock and they haven't even begun to feel the pain yet. They want to wake up and find it is all a dream, they are still in that stage. I dread that question and I never answer it. People ask 'Are you over it now?', like it is a bout of flu; you are never over it. You simply find a new normal – you will never be normal again in what was normal – and it takes a long time, at least two years ... grief is a journey of constructing a new life without the person you have lost and in the beginning, you don't want that new life – you want the old one back.

5

Divorce: the loss of a love,

the death of a relationship

Divorce is the most stressful experience after the death of a partner. It is very painful, far more disrupting than anyone who has not gone through it can imagine. 'I believed divorce would solve my problems; but now I realise that it solved one, but produced a dozen more.' These words, shared in tears by a young woman after ten years of marriage and three children, sum up the feelings of many divorcees.

Why is it so painful? There are many reasons, but the main one is probably the width of its effects. Divorce doesn't just affect the couple, but everyone to whom they are closely related; their children, their church family, their close relations, their friends and God. 'When we separated, I lost not only a wife, but also my children, my friends, my church ... all of a sudden, I realised I was deprived of the most meaningful people in my life.' Divorce is an emotional earthquake, shaking the very foundations of the building that is our identity and our self-esteem.

One of the leading experts on the subject, Judith S. Wallerstein, summarises the disrupting and wide-reaching effects of divorce: 'All breaking brings forth side effects which reach not only the couple involved, but the whole of society. Each divorce is the death of a little civilisation.'[41]

Divorce has much in common with the death of a loved person and the subsequent bereavement is very similar. The grief of divorce follows a pattern that is almost identical to the stages covered in chapter 1. Nonetheless, we need to devote a specific section to the bereavement caused by the break-up of a relationship because it has some distinctive features.

- Unlike conventional bereavement, the pain of the divorced is deliberately caused by the closest person to them. Anger therefore becomes a central issue in this kind of grief.
- There is always an element of blame in divorce which is far more intense than in conventional bereavement. Guilt and a sense of personal failure are outstanding here.
- Nobody is prepared for divorce. We all know how to behave at a funeral or the bedside of a sick person. Nobody prepared us for the trauma of the separation. Those bereaved by divorce feel overwhelmingly lost, confused, full of doubts and questions that they don't dare to ask.
- Divorce often means going on seeing the partner, because of the children. Death would be easier to endure 'because you don't see them any more.'

Consequently, recovery from the grief of divorce is messy and complicated. Nevertheless we can distinguish three overlapping stages with their own traits. Like the grief after death, the process is not linear but full of relapses: going up and down is quite a normal feature in any bereavement, but especially so in the loss of a child and divorce. In this case it is more accentuated because a break-up process, even when divorce is already set in motion, can be full of movements forward and backward, reuniting and separating before the final split. And so the length of the mourning here is considerably longer than in

---

[41] Judith S. Wallerstein, *'Second opportunities'*, 1989, quoted by Dr Luis Rojas Marcos, La pareja rota (*The broken couple*), Espasa Calpe, Madid 2003, 137

the non-complicated bereavement after death. An average of three to four years is required for a minimum healing of the wounds after the actual separation.

These are the most typical stages:

- Confusion
- Loneliness and isolation
- Adjustment and growth

Confusion: the emotional chaos after divorce

In the first weeks or months after the break-up the couple feels, above all, disoriented and chaotic. It is an emotional turmoil, with ideas, feelings and reactions all mixed up. They cannot believe that it is true. 'This can't happen to me.' They can't grasp the reality of the situation and this emotional reaction allows them to escape from the anguish.

This stage lasts about one year. Its main features are encapsulated in the words of an author of a major book on the subject: 'Divorce is an emotional bombshell. It almost invariably turns out to be far harder for both partners than either ever imagined. It crushes self-confidence, it rouses anger and guilt, it promotes insecurity, it complicates all interpersonal relationships'[42]. Unfortunately most divorced couples go through this experience.

Let us examine in more detail the emotional upheaval of this period.

- Great anguish expressed through physical symptoms. These are very similar to the first stage of bereavement and result from a high level of anguish. After the break-up, the spouses cannot sleep, they lose appetite and weight or else they eat in a compulsive way and gain weight; they cannot concentrate

---

[42] Andrew Cornes, *Divorce and Remarriage*, Hodder & Stoughton, quoted by Barry Seagren at *Evangelicals Now*, July 1995, page 9

on their work or do everyday tasks properly and they often cry. Headaches, breathing difficulties, dizziness, menstrual disorders, skin rashes and hair loss are also quite common among many other psychosomatic symptoms. This is the body showing its internal pain.

- Sometimes the reaction is surprisingly the opposite. One or both of the spouses initially feeds a sense of liberation and happiness straight after the separation. They say that they feel much better than before, they seem to have a lot of energy and enthusiasm; a certain euphoria is visible in their behaviour. This may be especially true for those couples with a long history of abuse, either verbal or physical, which was a source of great suffering to one of them. They consider the break-up as a real blessing –'the end of a hell'– and they regret that they did not separate much earlier. But this state does not last. All of a sudden, after days or weeks, any trivial event – a picture, a melody, a thought, even a certain smell – brings back memories of the relationship or of the partner and the 'happy liberated' spouse plunges into sadness, anguish and mourning.

- Enormous mood swings. Typically the divorced experience unexpected and intense mood swings. Their feelings change quickly and mix. Hate and anger may occur almost at the same time as love; strong rejection may quickly follow a deep desire to reunite. This ambivalence is a clear expression of a universal reality: love takes a long time to dwindle. It is like the ashes of a fire that are not easily extinguished. 'I am afraid to see him, because I fear that I will want to hold him,' said a 29-year-old woman whose husband abandoned her for another woman. These mood changes happen even when the divorce is seen as a real liberation, e.g. women who were physically abused, or in those couples that – theoretically – mutually agreed to divorce.

- A sense of failure and diminished self-esteem. One of the most common effects of divorce is to feel inadequate for having failed. Unlike bereavement, a marital break-up makes people question themselves a lot. Their ability to overcome this identity crisis becomes central in the resolution of the grief. The sense of failure may be very strong even in those cases when there are no objective reasons. An observer may find no logical explanations for the break-up, yet there is a pervasive feeling that 'I have failed in one of the most important exams in life.' 'Was I a good enough partner? Did I love enough? Am I still attractive?'

- This crisis becomes especially poignant in those cases when one of the spouses breaks the relationship without any previous period of conflict: 'We never had troubles; we were happy.' Even worse is the case when the break-up is because of a third party. 'What have I done wrong? What does she/he have that I don't?' All these thoughts damage the self-esteem and provoke a long-lasting crisis marked by insecurity and lack of self-confidence. I remember a man who, in the process of separation, started stuttering. He had never done it before, but now his insecurity was so intense as to be expressed through his speech.

- Guilt feelings. These are intertwined with low self-esteem. Remember they are a frequent, almost normal, symptom of bereavement. They release the pain of the loss. Associated with them is a need to reconsider the relationship over and over again, in order to discover 'what really happened.' This is not bad in itself because finding a satisfactory explanation for the separation is an essential requisite for the recovery. However, when the guilt feelings are very intense or the person becomes obsessive with this 'reconsideration of the past', this may be a symptom of clinical depression and medical treatment is necessary.

- A sense of anxiety and despair. The person finds themselves in a situation of uncertainty. Many doubts dominate their thoughts: fear of the future, of financial needs, of rejection by friends or church, of being morally condemned, fear 'that life is over.' Besides these future uncertainties, the present challenges are a source of stress too. The divorced person has to face many responsibilities that, previously, were shared. These changes are so overwhelming that they usually feel they are not in control of the situation. Then the person feels so vulnerable that they feel safer being away from people. This is why they withdraw which increases the anxiety and sense of loss.

Isolation and loneliness: the social effects of divorce

After this initial period of confusion and emotional upheaval, most couples that separate go through a period of loneliness and isolation which lasts from one to two years. Whereas the disturbances in the first months were more emotional and physical, now the social effects of divorce predominate.

Why is this? Divorce involves relationships. Divorce is, in its very essence, the result of a disagreement. No wonder, then, that the occurrence of tensions and quarrels is a frequent by-product. It is unusual to find a divorced couple where the different parts are able to keep a really harmonious relationship. Divorce may solve one problem, but it eventually creates a dozen more. This fact aggravates the grief of the spouses who struggle not only with the pain of the loss, but also with the tensions of endless interpersonal conflicts. In too many cases, divorce is the end of a relationship and the beginning of a war.

What are the main areas devastated by the separation?

Slowly the divorced person experiences good former relationships beginning to weaken. Friends or even family seem distant, and conflict over the legal and material affairs start. Nothing and nobody look the same any more. It is like starting life again, but alone. This is really tough. 'Can I trust people when the person I trusted most has failed me?' 'Who is going to accept or love me?' Guilt, shame, despair, all these feelings lead to withdrawal. 'I feel safe and comfortable alone.' This isolation is an unconscious way of protecting oneself from the supposed hostility of the world around: 'I'm going to retreat before others can reject me.'

Together with isolation the bereaved goes through a time of mourning and sadness. The sense of the loss becomes very intense now because they realise that the break-up is irreversible. In the first year or so there was still some hope that the separation would not last, specially for the spouse that was reluctant to break-up. But even those couples who agree to separate experience a deep sense of loss. It could not be otherwise. You shared the most intimate facets of your life for years with your partner: they were part of your identity, because 'a man will ... be united to his wife, and they will become one flesh' (Gen. 2:24). The original word in Hebrew for 'being united' means to glue, in such a way that when you separate the parts you have fastened, inevitably some are damaged.

After the break-up, many people are very surprised to discover that they feel lonelier and more unhappy than they did when their partner was still living with them – regardless of how good their marriage was. With the exception of those couples where there was severe physical abuse, most divorced people find their new situation of loneliness more unbearable than their marriage. This is one of the most striking facts that the experts have found at this stage of the grief process.

This mourning is not negative in itself. It has a very positive dimension because it helps the divorced come to terms with reality and admit that 'it's all over.' The opposite of mourning – the denial of reality – is a serious obstacle to progress towards adjustment and recovery, as we considered in pathological grief.

Depression is one of the possible complications of mourning. When the loss is unbearable, the divorced person falls into clinical depression with all the features we mentioned in chapter 2. Depression is, ultimately, the response of a heart that feels powerless to accept the reality. The divorced person feels unable to cope with life. Sometimes suicidal ideas may appear and medical help is necessary.

Wrong decisions and behavioural disorders are another complication of this stage. A quick remarriage, sexual promiscuity, alcohol or substance abuse are possible problems for anyone who is unable to accept the reality of a new life.

Resentment and hate have been present, in some degree, throughout the whole process. In the first months, however, they were countered by the hope of possible reconciliation. There was still more love than hate, at least affection. But now, at this later stage, the negative feelings are strong and predominate over the remainders of affection. Those involved feel angry, humiliated and rejected. The wounds are very deep and wide open. There is a vivid sense that 'what they did to me is totally unfair; I didn't deserve it and I'll never forget how badly I was treated.'

Anger reaches one of its peaks when the partner feels 'robbed' of their children: for example on the weekends or during the holiday periods when the partner who has got custody of the children has to be separated from them. The partner who has to renounce everyday contact with their children, except for strictly regulated periods, may feel similar anger. This reaction, of anger and loneliness equally mixed, is more intense when divorce is the result of adultery: one of the partners leaving home to be together with someone else. The abandoned spouse feels that they have lost not only the spouse, but also their children. On top of all this, the presence of someone new participating in their care and even education becomes unbearable to the abandoned parent and stirs up great resentment.

How is anger managed? Apparently divorce is the ceasefire of a lost battle, marriage. But in fact the battle often continues in different ways where the former spouses display a wide range of resources to win: lawyers, relatives, neighbours, church members etc. Consequently, the management of anger is one of the key points in the counselling of the bereaved by divorce. Two Bible texts which help us to face this painful issue in a very practical way:

'Do not repay anyone evil for evil … If it is possible, as far as it depends on you, live at peace with everyone. Do not take revenge, my friends, but leave room for God's wrath …' (Rom. 12:17-19).

'Bear with each other and forgive whatever grievances you may have against one another. Forgive as the Lord forgave you' (Col. 3:13).

According to these verses, two consecutive steps are necessary for a Christian to manage anger properly.

'Don't seek revenge': avoid any destructive attitudes or behaviour towards your former partner. Revenge is always poisonous for those near you and, eventually, also for yourself. Yet this is almost a natural reaction, especially in ways which are apparently harmless like indifference. Be careful with attitudes such as, 'This person has died to me, I will never speak to them again.' George Bernard Shaw said: 'The worst sin against your neighbour is not to hate them, but to be indifferent towards them.'

One of the saddest experiences I recall as a psychiatrist – after 25 years in the profession – is a trial which I was required to attend as a legal expert. A Christian couple had divorced and they were battling for the custody of their children. I will never forget the day of the trial when they had to meet face to face: the accusations, the slanders and, above all, the hatred you could read in their eyes made a memorable impact on me. How is it possible for two people, supposedly Christians, who once loved each other and promised faithfulness forever, to hate each other so much? How true that in all wars there are only losers and losses. The Bible warns us of the boomerang effect of these disputes: 'If you keep on biting and devouring each other, watch out or you will be destroyed by each other' (Gal. 5:15).

Sometimes the offended partner may actively seek revenge, clearly determined to destroy the other. These *destructive behaviours* can vary from the subtle manipulation of children as weapons to verbal or even physical aggression. It is amazing to discover the cruelty that the divorced can show towards their former spouses. An appalling number of women are killed or severely injured by their partners in our Western countries, to the point that it has become one of the main concerns for the authorities.

Because revenge is almost a spontaneous reaction in our fallen nature – you can observe some forms of naïve revenge in children! – the first step to manage anger is *self-control*. Don't let your impulses win. Don't allow your tongue or hands to work faster than your head. It isn't easy but remember that self-control is one of the Spirit's fruits. You are not asked for a natural reaction, but a supernatural one, with God's help.

Real forgiveness is the second requisite for managing anger properly. There are some frequent misunderstandings about forgiveness, so I would like to consider its main features according to the Scripture:

- Forgiveness is not necessarily mutual; it may be one-sided. I can – and must – forgive although the other person is reluctant to forgive or to be forgiven. Sometimes, they don't even know that we have forgiven them. This was the case of Jesus on the cross when – being about to die – he cried: 'Father, forgive them, for they do not know what they are doing' (Lk. 23:34). We must be ready to forgive although we are not asked to.
- Forgiveness requires our utmost efforts to be at peace with the other. This peaceful attitude does not necessarily imply the restoration of the relationship. This is always a desirable outcome, but isn't always possible. The disputing parties are not required to be friends again, but simply to live in peace. Paul recognises that even this is not always possible, but clearly states our part in the responsibility: 'as far as it depends on you'. That means that you have to try to be at peace with everybody, including your former spouse.
- Forgiveness implies the removal of all the negative feelings and thoughts about the other. It is like a wound healing; at first the wound is wide open, bleeding easily and exquisitely painful to the touch. But once it has become a scar, it doesn't hurt any more. Forgiving is like turning open wounds into scars – no more hostility or destructive behaviour. The memory of the painful experience is there, but the memory does not evoke negative feelings. Forgiving does not require forgetting and the scar remains. We cannot erase memories from our minds, but we can – and must – remove the poison from these memories.
- Real forgiveness can take a long time. The willingness to forgive may be an instant decision, but the actual forgiveness

may be long and costly. Remember the case of Joseph in the Old Testament. He amazingly forgave his brothers, but not before a long process – probably months – of struggling with his own reactions. It is important that you clearly say: 'I am determined to forgive you, although the healing of my wounds may take a much longer time.' With the exception of a minority who keep resentment forever, in most divorced couples the fire of hatred dwindles and gives place to healthier attitudes. As a matter of fact, the experts point out that – several years after divorce – the majority of them would help each other in an emergency situation.

Someone said that forgiveness is the best way to get rid of your enemies! We could apply this sentence to divorce and say: forgiveness is the best way to get rid of your anger and resentment towards the former spouse. In the bereavement caused by a break-up, forgiveness is a necessary ingredient for recovery.

Adjustment and growth

Following a divorce, the relationship cannot be reconstructed, but the pieces of your identity and self-esteem can be reassembled. This is the main purpose of this third stage: to help the divorced person face life with new strength, new attitudes and new goals.

Marks of a good adjustment

How do we evaluate the progress in the adjustment process? In the same way that we saw several signs of recovery after the death of a loved one, here we have certain criteria. The following traits show a good adjustment:

- *Acceptance*. The divorced person is able to face honestly the reality of life without their partner. They are fully aware of their new status in life. The sense of loss is not crippling any more. Acceptance means the awareness that in all circumstances, God can turn evil into good.

- *Adaptation*. The divorced is able to face the demands of everyday life without the spouse. The capacity to function socially without the help of the mate is a sign of good adjustment, in the simpler areas like the daily routines to the more complex ones like learning to be a single parent, either living apart from the children or as a one-parent family.
- *Explanation*. The bereaved always need a reasonable explanation of how and why it all happened. Finding reasons for the loss is essential to recovery. This explanation must be satisfactory from a subjective viewpoint. It helps to discover mistakes you have made, but also relieves false guilt feelings about mistakes you have not made.
- *Anger under control*. This implies all the steps mentioned earlier: don't seek revenge, don't be destructive, don't blame others, fight self-pity, and be ready to forgive. When all these features are present in your heart and mind, the recovery is well under way.
- *Is time the great healer?* How long does it take to heal the wounds? When is the grief caused by divorce over? This varies according to these factors; the circumstances of the separation, personality of the divorced, help available etc. Today most researchers agree that three to four years is the average time for a normal, healthy person to work out the problems after the actual break-up. But the wounds don't always make a proper scar. It is not unusual for the divorced to feel deeply wounded and even incapacitated after ten years. This is specially the case of the spouses who were abandoned by their partner without any apparent reason or for someone else.

The following comment from a 53-year-old is a good illustration of this difficulty in completely overcoming the pain of divorce: 'I have had relationships that lasted longer and were more serious than my marriage. Yet breaking off any of them has never involved the pain of my divorce ... There is a bigger sense of failure. The pain still hangs around me, twenty years later.'

Anna Raeburn, an expert on the subject, said: 'It is usual to think of divorce as a single event which will inevitably affect everyone in proximity for a while, but then life will go on, and time heals all wounds. The reality is that, psychologically, divorce is a chain which clinks and rattles at the ankles, and be it ever so long, does not let you go.'[43]

Resources for help: family, friends and church

During the process of the separation the person needs not only personal, emotional support but also practical help. There are many new challenges and practical decisions; perhaps a new house, money problems, taking care of small children, finding the right lawyers, getting a job etc. This is why the divorced need a lot of support, especially initially. The main resources here are similar to those of conventional bereavement; family, close friends and the local church.

- *Family* – the parents and siblings of the divorcee. Their reaction may vary from total support to open opposition to the marriage break-up. Their attitude will probably depend on the causes of the separation. Obviously the reaction will not be the same towards a man who leaves his wife and three children to go to live with another woman as with the spouses who separate because of 'incompatible personalities'. Divorce is usually the outcome of a complex process with more than one cause. We should avoid simple interpretations. In any case, regardless of the causes, support from parents and siblings is vitally important because they are the main source of affection during this period of grief. Probably no one else is nearer.

However, one word of clarification is necessary here: to support is not the same as to agree with. Parents may clearly

---

[43] *Evangelicals Now*

disagree with the decision and say so. They have the right to. But this disagreement should not exclude the warmth, acceptance and sympathy that their child so desperately needs. Disagreeing with the decision does not imply rejecting the person. This is one of the common mistakes made not only by parents, but also by Christians.

Remember Jesus' example: he openly condemned any behaviour which was ethically wrong, but he had a tender heart and showed great love for the individual regardless of their ethical condition. His encounter with the Samaritan woman is a good example. Jesus clearly points out her irregular marital situation – she was living with a man – but at the same time he displayed an amazing love and understanding towards her. The impact of such unconditional acceptance is seen by the results: 'Many of the Samaritans from that town believed in him because of the woman's testimony ... And because of his words many more became believers' (Jn. 4.39,41).

Also the divorcee should understand that support does not mean approval. Some people say: 'You don't understand me', simply because you don't approve of their behaviour. The bereaved by divorce should expect support and acceptance, but not always agreement.

- *Church*. The same principle applies to the greater family, the family of faith. People show a lot of sympathy for the bereaved through death, but easily blame those suffering from a marriage break-up. We should remember that one of the favourite strategies of the devil is to make church members become amateur judges. We are too fond of treating people judgementally in society in general and within the church in particular. Divorced people are lonely, insecure and afraid. The church can help – and condemnation is not the best way to do so. When people are feeling terrible about themselves, don't make them feel worse!

In more positive terms, what can the church offer?

Above all, *grace*. Grace is the most distinctive contribution that the church can make to those afflicted by divorce. In his excellent book *What's so amazing about grace?* Philip Yancey quotes Gordon MacDonald: 'The world can do almost anything as well as or better than the church ... There is only one thing the world cannot do. It cannot offer grace.'[44]

Grace is the remedy that Jesus gave us one day to forgive all our sins. But grace is also the balm that he continues to give us each day to bear with one another in love (see Eph. 4:2) and to 'Carry each other's burdens' (Gal. 6:2). Grace is the supernatural strength that enables us to 'Accept one another ... just as Christ accepted you' (Rom.15:7). Grace means 'wrapping the towel round your waist' rather than drawing the sword. Grace should be the hallmark of a community of forgiven sinners: the church is not a community of righteous people who rarely sin, but a community of sinners where grace is abounding.

One of the most moving experiences within the Christian community is the process of encouraging, building up and restoring those whose life is torn into pieces because of divorce. We greatly need to develop a pastoral heart towards those who often feel like the psalmist: 'My heart is blighted and withered like grass; ... I am like a desert owl, like an owl among the ruins ... I have become like a bird alone on a roof' (Ps. 102:4,6,7). To those who have lost their closest person, we can offer the warmth and support of the family of faith.

Grace is love in action. It is striking to discover that there are fifty commandments or exhortations in the New Testament containing the expression 'one to another': love, comfort, encourage, serve, bear, forgive and many other activities which reflect the grace of Christ. Those bereaved by divorce should experience the grace of Christ from their own fellowship with the Lord; but they also need to feel the grace of their spiritual family in all these practical ways.

---

[44] Philip Yancey, *What's so amazing about grace?* (Michigan: Zondervan Publishing House, 1997) 15

But Christ's grace can never be a 'cheap grace', to use the well-known expression of Dietrich Bonhoeffer. Cheap grace declares right what is wrong; overlooks sin and, in the name of tolerance, accepts any behaviour, even those which are openly against God's will. Cheap grace clings to the words of Jesus to the adulterous woman '… neither do I condemn you', but neglects the last part, 'Go now and leave your life of sin' (Jn. 8:11). The costly grace of Christ forgives every sinner, but does not approve of sin. The reality is that God hates divorce and it afflicts him so much that he said:

> You flood the LORD's altar with tears. You weep and wail because he no longer pays attention … You ask, "Why?" It is because the LORD is acting as the witness between you and the wife of your youth, because you have broken faith with her, though she is your partner, the wife of your marriage covenant … So guard yourself in your spirit, and do not break faith with the wife of your youth. "I hate divorce," says the LORD (Mal. 2:13-16a).

Sometimes divorce is clearly the result of sin in one of the partners and the church cannot overlook this reality. A local church cannot happily welcome a man who has left his wife and children because of a relationship with another woman or vice versa. There are some cases when a clear awareness of sin – that is, repentance – is a necessary ingredient for a full restoration of the divorced person. The prodigal son was welcomed and happily received in his father's house; but before this he showed an unmistakable attitude of repentance: 'Father, I have sinned against heaven and against you (Lk. 15:18). Notice that the words discipline and disciple have the same root which is 'to learn'. One cannot be a good disciple if there is no discipline. The church has the right and the duty to offer grace to the divorced, a grace which forgives and accepts but also exhorts and disciplines when the case demands so.

* * *

Jennifer Rees Larcombe is a well-known speaker and writer, and when her husband left her, she had to contend not only with her private grief but the public reaction.

Jennifer Rees Larcombe

How did you feel when your husband left?

Absolutely lost, done for, because I always relied on him. I felt I couldn't cope at all ... my son helped me open a bank account, which I hadn't had before ... I had no idea how that worked, he helped me to do all the bills, the direct debits, the mortgage, all those sort of things. I was also looking after my mother-in-law, who was living with us. She was desperately distressed. I think it helped me to have her, because I had someone to look after, to focus my thoughts. The day he went, I cleared out the garage and I never stopped for the next month, clearing out cupboards, spring-cleaning, because I couldn't cope. The chaos in my life was too big. I couldn't do anything about that, but I had to have little things I could do, like the kitchen cupboards, that I could control. I learnt how to cope with all the office things, I didn't stop night or day. I don't think I cried, I was keeping myself together for the children and my mother-in-law. None of the children were at home any longer – that was one of the worst things: my youngest son had left two weeks before for University and that was gutting enough in itself – but fortunately because of Mother-in-law I wasn't completely on my own.

I think there are certain things that make it worse than a bereavement ... one is that you don't have the feeling of comfort, knowing the one you love is safely in heaven waiting for you ... they are alive and happy with someone else. And you don't have the comfort of everyone writing lovely letters saying 'he was so lovely, he helped me so much...' All you hear is either people saying awful things about him, 'I always did think he was no good,' which you don't want to hear, because he is the person you chose to love most in the world – or you have people saying, ' He wasn't as bad as you are trying to make out.' That is hard too, because they are almost aggressively on his side, crushing you. And you don't have the comfort of the financial support that a widow gets: they get a widow's pension, and insurances and things like that, so you are suddenly in terrible financial straits. You are probably going to have to sell your home because you have to split the money and one of the hardest parts is the financial situation – and you don't have the love and support of Christian people. If your husband dies, everyone is around loving you and that does carry you through... What you have in this case is people backing off in terrible embarrassment, they don't know what to say so they disappear. I know that happens with death too. And you have people saying 'I am not going to take sides' so they drop you both ... and you do have a lot of condemnation – you have a sense of shame within you because your marriage has failed and that makes you feel like hiding rather than going to church so you hide away a bit and you would be amazed at the amount of condemnation you get ... I found no condemnation with non-Christians – they were nice – it was Christian people. I had a lot of awful letters from people ... being a public figure, having written a lot of books on other things, and they would say 'I am sure it was because you were healed' or 'It was because you spoke in public or you wrote books' and 'don't you think you should have done this' and 'I hope you are repenting because of that' ... and actually you are repenting, and you really don't need to have it thrown at you again and again because Jesus doesn't do that ...

Is this because people really don't want to believe this happens to Christians?

Yes ... my very best friend said to me, 'this wouldn't have happened if you had been closer to the Lord' but the thing is when your marriage breaks up that you actually agree with them. You think, 'I should have done this or that, I could have loved him more.' it is how you feel, but on the other hand no one has had a perfect marriage and you can never look back on a marriage and think 'I was perfect' ... and you can always love someone more. You have got no funeral, no grave, no end ... and you always hope that maybe he will come back. Even now I think all the time, he might come back.

I couldn't have lived without God ... I don't know how anyone could go through it without him. I think one of the hardest things is that being angry gives you a protection – it covers you round, it carries you through, gives you energy, it gives you fight, but when you are trying to be forgiving and not being angry, it makes it harder, but still it is right to be forgiving. It makes you vulnerable and you don't want to be vulnerable – it is much easier if you can say 'curse him'. You can't say that and I think that does make it harder ... people invariably try to make you work through the forgiveness thing too fast... in the month after he left, I received four different tapes of different sermons on forgiveness that people thought I should hear ... and I couldn't cope with them then. They were very good and I listened to them later but you cannot actually forgive until you have grieved and felt the pain, faced up to it and then let it go, but you can't be rushed into it.

I had two or three friends who never minded listening, one particular friend would be around and it didn't matter how many times I said something... she would come shopping with me or do gardening with me ... and another friend rang me up early each morning, because she knew I woke early, and it was so lovely – your whole life has been thrown up in the air and everything you relied on has gone and these were new things which were trustworthy ... a lot of people will do it for a while but then they consider you ought to be over it, and they withdraw totally, suddenly and arbitrarily. It always takes longer than you expect and much longer than other people think it should ... It is still happening now ... it is three years and I am fine sometimes and it will come over me again...

I think it is very hard for people to understand the grieving process, because it is so uneven. You can be fine at first, because you are numb, and you can be euphoric – you are so held by God and prayer. I was like that for six months, maybe a year... and then you go through the different stages. Christians find it very hard to cope with the angry stage, because they think 'she shouldn't be talking like that ... she should be loving, forgiving and accepting ... and they find it extremely hard to cope with the depressed stage ... because the depression often hits 18 months to two years after, when everyone thinks you are over it and you think you are and suddenly you can't believe the depth of it and by that time your friends have drifted back to real life again and they don't expect you to be still struggling. Other people say 'Stop crying' but what they mean is 'I can't cope with you crying.'

At the end of a big depression ... my GP said to me you won't get over this depression until you can let your husband go and I thought

... I don't want to let him go, I want him to come back ... and that was a big problem to me until I realised that often you hold onto the marriage that was – and I thought if he ever comes back he will be different and I will be different so we will have to start again from scratch. I had to let go of the marriage that had been. I wrote down all the things that I remembered – a sort of token of it – all the good and bad things – and I buried that. It was a symbolic letting go of the marriage that had been in order to be ready for a new one ...

The end of the grieving process is the place of acceptance and that is very hard to come to when you are a Christian ... it is accepting that what has happened has happened and you are going to move on in your life and you're not going to pester God to put the clocks back. But it is a long haul.

Helping children survive divorce

So far we have seen how painful divorce is for the spouses. But the amount of suffering caused by the separation of parents is far greater in the children. The research shows that the effects of divorce on them are more severe than on the parents and last much longer, usually a lifetime. Even with the most peaceful divorces, when parents continue to have a civilised contact between them and children are cared for and loved, children suffer the consequences.

Adults tend to believe that the suffering caused to children by divorce is clearly lesser than the suffering of living in a home with constant tension, so 'for their sake, it is better to divorce.' As a psychiatrist I cannot accept this claim. Actually, most of the time this is an excuse for the parents – a rationalisation – to justify their separation. I am not suggesting that a highly destructive marriage should be sustained at all costs for the sake of the children. I am simply saying that most parents who want to divorce are unaware of the tremendous, long-lasting effects that their separation will have on their children.

A special comment on guilt is necessary. Children have a tendency to feel guilty and blame themselves for anything that goes wrong; they feel guilty about their parents' quarrels and eventual break-up. This may lead them to attitudes of self-hatred and depression. They need to be reassured that they are not responsible for the trauma.

Children are hurt, whatever their age. Surprisingly, even at the teen years, they are harmed. You would expect a higher degree of emotional resistance as they grow up, but usually this is not the case. I was recently counselling a nineteen-year-old guy who was very affected by the separation of his parents: 'I *know* that I should be stronger, but I can't avoid *feeling* like a broken person. I feel like a rope being pulled from two poles and this makes me feel awful.' His words are a good summary of the profound injury children have to endure. Unlike their parents, children have genes from both sides. The separation splits them into two: mixed loyalties, misplaced guilt and internal emotional conflicts will continue for all their lives.

It is astonishing to know that two-thirds of the children lose all contact with one parent within five years of the divorce. This sad reality probably explains the fact that, as the experts point out, the death of a parent does not have the same adverse impact on children as divorce does. The feeling that 'my father or mother is somewhere, still alive, but not caring for me' conveys an unbearable sense of loss.

One of the problems that comes as a surprise to the divorced is the negative reaction that children, especially teenagers, sometimes show towards a parent. This happens regardless of the initial feelings of a child. At the beginning they may openly support the decision. When the separation is just an idea, they may encourage one of the parents to separate. Even in the first days or weeks after the actual separation, they seem to be doing quite well.

But suddenly, a radical change happens and all the support is turned into blaming and reproaches. It is not unusual to find attitudes of overt hostility towards one parent, even rejection. This is an extremely painful experience. Often children blame one of the parents for the separation. To them, the problem is not as complex as the adults believe it is. For them there is a 'good' and a 'bad' parent. Sometimes their conclusion is very much influenced by the negative comments that one of the parents makes about the other. This is a perverse behaviour that, ultimately, hurts the child. No divorced parent should use this strategy.

If we had to summarise the best attitudes to help and encourage the children of divorce, we would suggest you should:

- Reassure your children that they will continue to be loved, cared for and supported, and do it. Be tolerant and patient with their adjustment. Don't forget that they are suffering. Don't neglect your children's emotional needs during this time when you are confused and disorganised. Avoid anything that could be interpreted as abandonment. Use the extended family of both parents, specially grandparents, to provide emotional support.
- Always be positive about their other parent. Don't make destructive comments about your former partner. Any negative remark makes the child feel that his attachments are dissolving, causes distrust and aggravates the pain. Don't use your children as pawns, whether for money, legal or custody rights or anything else. Don't use them as your counsellor or confidante. They cannot fulfil this role.
- Avoid changes in your children's routines. It is better for siblings to remain together, schools and the house they live in to remain the same. Let all their emotional energy be devoted to the adjustment and acceptance of the new family situation. Any further change will increase their anxiety.
- Try to keep lines of communication with them. Children need desperately to express their feelings. The time you devote to listening to them and sharing any thoughts or emotions is invaluable. Children always get great reassurance – much more than adults may realise – from talking and being listened to. This is the best antidote against their insecurity and anxiety.

It is good to remember that the building which is the family may fall apart, but ultimately God continues to be the architect. Therefore God is able to build up the 'house' again even from the ruins of a broken family. Children from broken families can be healed, restored and used by a loving Father who tells us: 'How can I give you up? Can a mother forget the baby at her breast and have no compassion on the child she has borne? Though she may forget, I will not forget you! See, I have engraved you on the palm of my hands' (Hos. 11:8a and Is. 49:15,16).

Growth and hope: life springs up again

The final stage is growth: adjustment and recovery are not the end. Every crisis is also an opportunity to grow, divorce included. God is able to work for good in all things (see Rom. 8:28), including the undesired trauma of marital separation. Not that divorce is a personal triumph, an expression of your freedom to choose and change, as is often said today. Any growth which arises from the wish to put the ego first is deeply unbiblical. This pervasive humanist ideology holds a worldview which is exactly the opposite of the biblical principle that man is not the centre of his own life, but God is.

Emotional and spiritual growth should be the final outcome of divorce. The break-up of a marriage is painful; divorce is the end of a dear relationship, but it is not the end of life. There is hope for the future. I am not referring to a new relationship; while remarriage is a possibility for some, many others will refuse this option, at least for many years. What do I mean by hope? God can make sense of our lives, give meaning to them, in spite of our mistakes or our painful experiences. Even more, God is able to use us not only in spite of our past, but through it. In the same way that gold is refined in fire, our faith is tested in grief and all kinds of trials. The final outcome is a higher degree of maturity (1 Pet. 1: 6,7). This is true spiritually and emotionally. Don't regret your past sufferings, but try to discover the new ways that God may want to show you in the future. There are many dark 'whys' in our life that can only be understood under an illuminating 'what for?' It is only when we honestly search after God's purposes that we realise he is able to transform tragedies into stories with sense and a moral meaning. The very words of God in Isaiah 43:18,19 are the best balm to heal the wounds of the bereaved by the loss of divorce.

> Forget the former things;
>> do not dwell on the past.
> See, I am doing a new thing!
>> Now it springs up; do you not perceive it?
> I am making a way in the desert,
>> and streams in the wasteland.

* * *

Martin Ryder[45]

I was married for 13 years. I believed that I had a very good marriage; in fact, the last year of my marriage – I thought – was probably the best year that we had had. So it came as a bolt out of the blue when my wife announced that she wanted a separation.

Was there someone else involved? She said no. She said this marriage was not fulfilling, it wasn't what she wanted, she had been going to leave me the previous year, she said. In the end, you ask yourself – was I in a different marriage? Because my perception was not hers.

There were about three months between her saying she wanted to go and her actually going. You will do absolutely anything to make the person change their mind but the bottom line was – there is no bottom line. You don't throw away 13 years of marriage, especially not if you have young children. My children were aged eleven and nine at the time and absolutely nothing I said made any difference. You will offer everything ... if there is no one else involved – and she assured me there wasn't ... I offered to create some modus vivendi – there must be some way for us to live together, for the sake of the children, there was no need to traumatise them. I even offered, and I meant it, I will sleep in the garage if that is what it takes – but there was no bottom line. She had made up her mind that she was going to leave.

---

[45] Not his real name

Physical reactions – you feel sick in the stomach. You feel you have done something wrong, you feel terrified, you don't know what is going on around you, you are incredibly tearful, frustrated, angry and confused.

How do you make sense of this? When I got married, I joined a queue with a sign at the front of it that said 'Get married – stay together for ever'. After 13 years of standing in this queue, I discovered someone had switched the signs. I hadn't been in the queue for divorce and break-up. As a Christian, you start believing 'If I pray hard enough, talk to God, things will work out.' I started reading the Bible a lot more, praying a lot, throwing myself very much more into my faith. Part of that is bargaining with God – dear God, if I pray hard enough and if I read my Bible then will you please be nice to me? So how do you please God? Let's do some holy things ... If you read your Bible, especially the Old Testament, the vast majority of the Old Testament came out of the experience of captivity, where Israel longed for restoration, longed for Jerusalem to be rebuilt and for the captives to return. The whole of the New Testament is about reconciliation with God. Isn't it amazing that when someone has left you and you're in a bad place, every time you read your Bible it promises that good things will happen, your prayers will be answered and all will be well. I say that as a warning but a little corner of me doesn't want to dismiss it because all will be well. God is faithful. But at the time you start thinking – she's going to come back. Almost every day my Bible told me that it was going to be all right, things were going to be restored.

I was angry with God. I wouldn't say I am now, but there are still many things I can't make sense of and which I am learning to live with. As a Christian, you want to believe we live in a moral universe and that there are moral consequences. You want to believe that if you do good, good will happen to you and if you do bad, then you'll get a thunderbolt. The problem is it doesn't work that way, but you still try to rationalise it by saying 'Ah well, for unbelievers anything will go, but for us Christians, if we do good things, good things will happen.' But it isn't that simple. So I was very angry with God and very confused, but at the same time he was the only thing I had left to hold on to.

I had no time off work. My congregation [Martin was a pastor] were very understanding and very supportive. That is actually why I didn't have to take time off work or get any happy pills. I immediately plugged myself into professional help. By divine intervention or coincidence, however you want to look at it, I met a clinical psychiatrist, a wonderful Christian, who simply said: 'Come and see me, I think you and I should talk.' He made himself available to me every week for the best part of a year without any charge. I also had good friends who knew I was going to phone every night at 11 o'clock and I was going to moan down the phone and I was going to say 'Do you know what she did today? Do you know what she said? How could she do this? How could she say that?' Virtually every night – sometimes they would be falling asleep at the other end as I fulminated and got it off my chest. It went on for months, for as long as I needed it: one or two very good friends who simply listened – that's all – listened and went along with everything I said, no matter how preposterous it was. Because there are no answers, there are no explanations, you cannot explain why people do terrible things.

Forgiving was something that I used to wrestle with. On a scale of human existence, the break up of a marriage is no big deal, compared to Hitler gassing six million Jews. But it filled my horizon, the pain I was going through. Forgiveness is a very difficult thing to get a handle on – how do you know when you have forgiven someone? You certainly never forget. I would say I have forgiven my ex-wife and I no longer give her the power to hurt me.

The shock – you can't make sense of it – how do you make sense of what seems to be a senseless act of emotional violence? There's an element of how does God let this happen? I think I have found a way to live with those kinds of questions but at the same time you have to go in faith and that's not easy. If God could let this happen why bother believing in him? What is the point of faith? Looking back now, I can honestly say the point of faith is that without faith, how much more would you suffer carrying those sorts of burdens? Without people of faith and love round about me, would I have been able to cope? Without good Christian friends who were prepared to fall asleep at the end of the phone while I ranted and raved?

I like to think of myself as a nice guy. I'm a kind, caring person. I don't hurt small animals. I give money to charity. I'm kind to my parents. I never hit my children – I'm a nice guy. No, I'm not. When somebody does that to you, suddenly from deep within you, you find real anger, real bitterness. The most awful vindictive thoughts come into your mind, and I deeply resented her ability to draw out from me these terrible things. How dare you turn me into a very petty and hurtful person? You always know it is there but you don't see it face to face; you don't like to see the darker side of your nature.

To someone else going through the same situation, I would say, don't expect there to be any answers. One of the real tragedies is that the only thing you have to hope for is that the pain fades, you pick up your life and you learn to live again. I say that's a tragedy because at the time it is so appalling that you cannot conceive of that ever happening. I thought that 'If I can get over this then that will belittle it, demean it.' There is an element of wanting to be a tragic figure. You think –' If I committed suicide that would show everybody how awful this is.' It is an appalling tragedy but you do get over it. You can pick yourself up and live a normal life. It is your only hope, for your own peace of mind. You can't say this to someone – my friends didn't say to me – 'It's all right, one day you'll get over it' – they sat there and they listened and they prayed with me – you have to go through that process: depression, anger, bargaining, acceptance.

I was quite calculating about getting over it. I thought – I can't go on holding this door open for ever – emotionally I can't do that. You can't spend the rest of your life hoping this is going to happen. I decided I would give it a year. This was quite a while into it – I said to myself, 'If after a year she's hundreds of miles away, living with another man, then I will have to accept the marriage is over' and I had – for my own sanity – to move on, to allow myself to move on, to start forgetting. I didn't feel I could hold out for ever. What do you do with all these emotions? I put an awful lot of my energies into trying to be a good father. I immediately became – not quite obsessive – but certainly religious in keeping the house clean and making sure the ironing was done and keeping the school uniforms washed and pressed. Without fail every Sunday night the ironing board came out and the hoovering was done, regular as clockwork – things which I have now let slip quite dramatically! Partly it was punishment to myself but it was certainly also – where do I put my feelings of inadequacy and how do I make myself feel good about what [is] happening? And one of the ways was – Look, I'm a good father, I can keep a house and I can cook. 'I'll show her!' was probably going on at the back of my mind.

What's the long-term effect? There's probably an element of not wanting to give anyone the power to hurt me again, and I haven't remarried.

How do you walk when there is no light? Having been a Christian for 20 years, it is not easy to jack in. You don't suddenly wake up and say, 'Oh that's it, things have gone wrong, I'll jack it in.' Something within me knew – I don't know how this is going to work out and I feel I am in a living hell, this is a nightmare from which I don't think I am ever going to wake up – I've got adrenaline pumping around constantly, I feel sick, I feel lost, bewildered, hurt and confused, I feel useless and worthless – if someone prefers nothing instead of me then I must be worth less than nothing. That is what she said. 'Do you want to live with me?' 'No, I prefer nothing.' So if you prefer nothing to me, I'm less than nothing.

I still come back to the fact that something in you doesn't want to get out of it, because it is too horrendous. I used to think if there was a God, then he would decide that one partner was right and one partner was wrong and the one that was wrong would spontaneously implode, and I couldn't understand why that didn't happen. At the time there was no way on God's earth that I was ever going to say I forgive her – and to do so would have been a dreadful dishonesty to my humanity. God gives you tears, God gives you emotions, God gives you pain and hurt, these are part of your humanity and if you walk around when your wife or husband leaves you, saying 'this is the will of a loving Father – I must accept it' then you are living in cloud-cuckoo land. God has given you these emotional responses to be able to cope and one of the ways you cope is by being hurt, being angry, lashing out – these are ordinary human emotions. And if some Christian tells you, 'You must forgive them, you must sit down now and pray for your ex-partner,' maybe some people can do that but I suspect most people would simply be denying their humanity. They would be short-changing themselves as human beings and their Creator. I am able to pray for my ex-wife; I don't particularly want to, but with the children having prayers at night, we prayed for Mummy and I prayed for Mummy through gritted teeth because I didn't want to. You're very aware that the children are living with this broken-

ness ...You saw every day what she had done and having to negoti-
ate with her when they went to see her... it was devastating. Every
parent knows that when a child skins their knee, you hurt: the one
thing you want to do as a parent is to wave this magic wand and stop
the hurting. When it is your own partner who has inflicted this pain,
it is a million times harder to explain. If she died, you are not left with
the 'she chose to do this' and you don't have to go on negotiating
with her.

One friend wrote to me: 'Suffering and love are two great myster-
ies which the cross refuses to have separated, and we who profess to
follow Christ cannot dare to claim exemption from either if our work
and our witness is to be at all deep.'

There are no answers, and if anyone says to you, this is why it happened and this is what will happen – well, beware those who say,
peace, peace, when there is no peace. But there is a way to live with
the questions and now, looking back after seven years – and I would-
n't have dreamed of saying this at the time – now looking back, I look
at what God did in Jesus and it doesn't offer us the answers to everything and I believe what was going on in God sending Jesus – part of
it – is he was saying 'I will be with you and if you don't understand
what is going on, then as a token of the fact that I am with you I am
sending my only Son. I am going to let the world throw everything it
can at him, the most horrible evil that the world can find' I will throw
at my own Son – and this is my pledge to you until you do understand, until you are free of the limitations of these three dimensions,
of human body and mind, until you are with me. Because I know it is
inexplicable – and you cannot understand – here is my promise, my
promise is here in Jesus. That's what Paul was saying, 'If God gave
his only Son, then trust him. Even if you don't understand, then trust
him.'

I say that now but it meant nothing at the time. It was a theological statement that had no emotional impact or importance and folk
who say things like – this explains it, this is what God is saying to you
– pray this, do that – it isn't that easy. Sometimes you have to suffer.
Jesus on the cross said 'My God, my God, why have you abandoned
[sic] me?' Feeling abandoned is no bad thing if even God's own Son
was able to do it.

6

I see the rainbow rising:

comfort for the present, hope for the future

Is death the end of all? Is there another life after this life? Can faith change bereavement in any way? The answer to these questions will deeply affect our attitude to death. As we anticipated in chapter 1, faith in general and the Christian faith in particular play a crucial role in the course of bereavement. It is the balm that may change despair into hope, tears full of bitterness into confident mourning. Therefore we are dealing here not just with a theoretical discussion on diffused subjects, but with matters of life or death. If the teachings of the Bible are true – and we certainly believe so – they have consequences not only for our life here, but also for the afterlife.

Because our journey through grief would be incomplete without some words of hope, we shall devote this last chapter to the specific comfort which arises from Christian faith. Christianity makes a big difference to the grieving person because it provides solid answers to the most poignant questions the bereaved face:

- Why did God allow it?
- Is death an absurdity or it has some meaning and purpose?
- How can some people say that dying is gain?

- What are the differences between mere immortality and the resurrection?
- What will life in heaven be like?

Before we focus our attention on these and other questions, we need to consider one thought which summarises all we are going to consider in this chapter: 'Blessed are those who mourn'. This sentence, one of the Beatitudes in the Sermon on the Mount, is quite an astonishing claim. It contains one of the many paradoxes of faith. How can a person who is grieving be 'very happy' at the same time? (The word 'blessed' in Greek – *makarios* – means 'happy'). In this revolutionary thought, Jesus gives us strong hints on how to understand the Christian perspective on mourning.

This Beatitude can be interpreted in three ways. Most commentators agree that the disciple mourns primarily for his own sin and unworthiness and also for the suffering in this world. These are its main meanings. Nevertheless, they do not exclude a literal interpretation which is perfectly compatible with the other two: blessed is the man who has experienced sorrow in all the bitter ways that life can bring.

We should note that the word used here for 'to mourn' is the strongest term for mourning in the Greek language. In the Old Testament the same word is applied to Jacob's grief when he thought that his son Joseph had died (Gen. 37:34). As William Barclay has put it: 'It is the kind of grief which takes such a hold of a man that it cannot be hid. It is not only the sorrow which brings an ache to the heart; it is the sorrow which brings unrestrainable tears to the eyes.'[46]

Let us examine the practical implications that this Beatitude has for the bereaved.

- Mourning is taken for granted. It is a natural and healthy way to express grief. Jesus does not rebuke the mourners, but calls them 'blessed'!

---

[46] William Barclay, *The Gospel of Matthew, vol. 1*, (Edinburgh: Saint Andrews Press, 1972), 88

- Mourning is considered to be desirable. It is included among a list of positive qualities of the character such as meekness, mercy, purity of heart and peacemaking.
- Mourning does not exclude happiness. We can be weeping at the loss of a loved one and yet, at the same time, keep inner peace or even joy (as we shall see later).
- The happiness of the mourner is deeper than a feeling. It is a profound conviction that 'neither death ... nor anything else in all creation, will be able to separate us from the love of God that is in Christ Jesus' (Rom. 8:38,39).
- The blessing or happiness of the mourner come from the fact that they will be comforted. Receiving comfort is the key that changes something apparently negative – sadness, grief – into a blessing.

Now we need to go a step further and answer another question. In which sense is the mourner blessed? In what practical ways can the experience of mourning make them happy? Grief can bring two benefits: first, an opportunity to experience, more than at any other time, the love and empathy of others. Secondly, it is an opportunity to experience the compassion and love of God, to meet him in a personal and fresh way. Many people have discovered a totally new God in times of great distress. Therefore, without mourning, we would miss this unique dimension of comfort.

> I walked a mile with Pleasure,
> She chattered all the way,
> But left me none the wiser
> For all she had to say.
>
> I walked a mile with sorrow,
> And ne'er a word said she,
> But, oh, the things I learned from her
> When sorrow walked with me![47]

---

[47] Quoted by William Barclay, *The Gospel of Matthew, vol. 1*, (Edinburgh: Saint Andrews Press, 1972), 88

So even in the midst of grief, Christians can boldly say that they are 'happy'. They are happy because they are able to view a totally different face of death. It is no longer the disgusting, frightening side of it, but the radiant perspective on life after death which Christ made available for us. Let us discover these realities that sustain our hope and become a soothing balm in our bereavement.

1 Death has a meaning and a purpose

'Why?' 'What for?' These are usually the first words that come to our minds when we face any kind of suffering, including death. We seek for reasons and for meaning in situations which look absurd or undeserved. This reaction is very understandable: when we get answers, even if they are not complete ones, our pain and perplexity are relieved. A certain degree of understanding of the nature of death is a necessary ingredient in the grief process. The more insight we get, the better the prognosis is for the bereavement. Hence the importance of providing the grieving person with appropriate answers about death and the life after death.

We need to start with some brief considerations on the meaning of death. Certainly we cannot have a specific answer to every death. Only God knows the details behind each particular case. But we do indeed have a good amount of knowledge about the reasons and purpose of death as a human reality. According to the teaching of the Bible, we learn that:

Death is not a natural event, but a foreign body. This may be surprising to some people. Most people consider death as something natural, as natural as life itself. Human death is not natural in the sense that it did not exist in God's creation. It was not part of his original intention for humankind. As John Stott puts it, 'God seems to have intended for human image-bearers a more noble end, akin perhaps to the "translation" which Enoch and Elijah experienced, and to the "transformation" which will take place in those who are alive when Jesus comes'.[48]

So death came as an unwanted intrusion into God's world. How and why did this happen?

Death is the result of sin. 'For the wages of sin is death, but the gift of God is eternal life in Christ Jesus ...' (Rom. 6:23). The Scripture clearly links these two undesired realities: sin and death. This does not mean that every single death is the result of a specific sin. Not at all. It refers to the origin and the ultimate cause of death. Death entered the world when the first man, Adam, chose to be independent from God and to live his own life apart from his Creator. This deliberate separation from God was an act of rebellion and is the very core of sin. Its results were devastating; they affected all the areas of human life. For this reason we find troubles in our minds, in our relationships, in nature and so on. The Bible describes this abnormal situation very accurately: '... the whole creation has been groaning as in the pains of childbirth right up to the present time ... we ourselves ... groan inwardly as we wait eagerly ... the redemption of our bodies' (Rom. 8:22,23). Death is, thus, a divine judgement on human disobedience.

Death is more than a physical fact. The Scripture speaks of three kinds of death. They are all the consequence of sin. There is *physical death* which is the separation of the soul from the body. There is *spiritual death* which is the separation of the soul from God. Finally, *eternal death* which is the separation of both soul and body from God for ever. In this sense, there is a remarkable difference between the death of animals – just a physical fact – and human death. Death is not the mere ending of some biological processes, as the materialist mind of our day claims. In the same way that human sexuality is not merely a body function, but has a deeper purpose, death also has an existential meaning behind it. Death means something. For this reason, bereavement is always a fertile ground for considering the spiritual dimensions of both life and death.

---

[48] John Stott, *The cross of Christ* (Leicester: IVP, 1986), 65

Death is the 'megaphone' that warns us of a deep disease. When a machine is not working properly, a red light warns us that it needs to be repaired. In a similar way, death is the main symptom of a disease that requires appropriate treatment. It is not a physical ailment, but this moral and spiritual condition that we call sin.

Therefore, death, with all its horror, gives us an opportunity – perhaps the main one – to reflect on the meaning of this life, with all its transcendental questions. It is in times of bereavement – especially when death has touched our loved ones – that we are all challenged with a profound reality: 'Am I ready to leave?'

Sooner or later each one of us is confronted with the same situation as king Hezekiah: 'This is what the LORD says: Put your house in order, because you are going to die; you will not recover [from your illness]' (Is. 38:1). Certainly it is not always so blunt and clear as Hezekiahs' experience, but God usually speaks to us in periods of grief. A crisis usually brings forth an opportunity. Suffering and death can be the instrument of God in making us realise that our sickness – sin – requires treatment.

In a suffering world, death is an act of mercy. So far we have seen that death is inevitable because of its penal dimension: it is God's just reward to human disobedience. But this explanation alone would be incomplete and also could give us a wrong picture of God's character. When God's creation was spoiled with sin, evil and all kinds of suffering became predominant on earth. Life was such a source of suffering that God himself, for a moment, planned to wipe humanity from the earth as the best solution to so much evil:

> the LORD saw how great man's wickedness on the earth had become, and that every inclination of the thoughts of his heart was only evil all the time. The LORD was grieved that he had made man on the earth, and his heart was filled with pain. So the LORD said, 'I will wipe mankind ... from the face of the earth ... for I am grieved that I have made them' (Gen. 6:5-7).

Can you think of a worse punishment than living for ever in this terrible world? Not a few people consider their life a real hell. No wonder there is a rise in the number of suicides. No wonder that euthanasia finds a favourable climate of opinion in many countries. Living for ever – or even for a long time – on this earth would be unbearable to most people. Job, the expert on suffering and death, describes human life in a very vivid way: 'Man born of woman is of few days and full of trouble' (Job 14:1). Surely it is not by chance that both realities go together: overwhelmed by a lot of trouble, our days are fortunately few. In other words, God in his mercy provided an expiry date to life on earth.

'*But God meant it for good.*' Many times we have no answer to the question 'Why did God allow such a death?' However, we are given certain answers in the Bible which are very uplifting in times of grief. One of these certainties is God's power to turn tragedies into meaningful stories. The lives of Naomi and Ruth in the Old Testament are a striking example of this transformation. They experienced severe losses and bereavement. Naomi lost her husband and her two sons. Ruth, her daughter-in-law, became a widow when she was quite young. They were both lonely, in a foreign land, apparently abandoned by God. Naomi complained bitterly and expressed the deep anguish of her soul. Their grief was very intense. Truly sometimes we just cannot understand 'why'.

But this was only the first chapter in the book of their life. Most tragedies have a second part which shows a precious reality: God is in control; nothing happens in our life outside of his knowledge and ultimately 'in all things [he] works for the good of those who love him ...' (Rom. 8:28). Ruth experienced God's power to restore her through her marriage with Boaz. She had come to know the secret of experiencing God's faithfulness: 'you have come to take refuge [under God's wings]' (Ruth 2:12). In this case God came to meet her greatest need (a widow in those days was in a very desperate situation). It is certainly not always like this; sometimes it is difficult to see God's providence in the dark night of crisis; but one thing is sure: God is able and willing to '[make] a way in the desert and streams in the wasteland' (Is. 43:19). Our life may be full of sad events, grief or losses. But with Joseph we can confidently say: 'You intended to harm me, but God intended it for good' (Gen. 50:20).

2 Death was defeated: 'You shall never die

'... so that by his death he [Jesus] might destroy him who holds the power of death – that is, the devil – and free those who all their lives were held in slavery by their fear of death' (Heb. 2:14,15).

In spite of all the reasons mentioned above, death continues to be unpleasant and even repulsive. Our normal reaction is to fear and reject it. In fact, the fear of personal death is almost universal. The Bible calls it 'The last enemy to be destroyed ...' (1 Cor. 15:26). The tears of Jesus before the tomb of Lazarus – '... he was deeply moved in spirit and troubled' (Jn. 11:33b) – certainly expressed pain, but also his deep rejection of this unnatural separation. Even God the Father shows a similar feeling in some Old Testament texts, for example in Psalm 116:15: 'Precious in the sight of the lord is the death of his saints.' The word 'precious' can also be translated by 'costly', showing us how painful this unnatural phenomenon is to our Creator who designed us to live for ever.

But God, who was about to destroy humanity altogether as we just saw, in his mercy decided to provide us with something far better than a mere shortening of our days on earth. He gave us the possibility of a new life – a new heaven and a new earth where 'No longer will violence be heard ... nor ruin or destruction ... [for] the LORD will be your everlasting light, and your days of sorrow will end' (Is. 60:18, 20). This decision to provide another opportunity for us to live in a world without death is the essence of the Christian message, the good news of eternal life in Christ.

There are three basic ideas we need to know about the victory of Jesus over death. As we consider them, we will be reaching the core of the gospel. Its implications are far reaching and long-lasting. If we understand what the Bible teaches on death at this very point – and believe it – then the consequences are revolutionary; we cannot remain the same and it will deeply affect our grief process.

The death of Jesus on the cross makes the 'snake' harmless

> The apostle Paul wrote defiantly: '"Where, O death, is your victory? Where, O death, is your sting?" The sting of death is sin … But thanks be to God! He gives us the victory through our Lord Jesus Christ' (1 Cor. 15:55,57).

Death contains a sting which is where all its poison and danger lies. Sin is what turns death poisonous because it makes it for ever, eternal. If this sting could be neutralised, then death would be harmless. This is exactly what Christ did: he died for us and he took away our sins: '… our Saviour, Christ Jesus, … has destroyed death and has brought life and immortality …' (2 Tim. 1:10).

Because death has lost its power to harm, we are not terrified by it any more. In Christ we have a different view on this poignant enemy. A new window is opened before our eyes to show us a luminous landscape with a totally different perspective. Death is still an enemy, but it is a *defeated* enemy.

We could thus say, that the day Jesus rose from the dead, it was the 'day when death died'.[49] With such an event, the bereaved may experience a dramatic change in their attitude because now death is not the end of everything. There is hope. There is a future.

---

[49] An expression used by Michael Green. This is the title of his book *The day death died* (Leicester: IVP, 1982). It is an excellent study on the resurrection of Jesus which we warmly recommend.

The resurrection of Jesus is the guarantee for our future life after death

How was this made possible? What foundation or security do we have to know it is true? Paul vigorously explains it to us: 'But Christ has indeed been raised from the dead, the firstfruits of those who have fallen asleep. For since death came through a man, the resurrection of the dead comes also through a man' (1 Cor. 15:.20,21).

Obviously Christ is called the 'firstfruits' of the harvest and 'the firstborn from the dead' because many others will follow afterwards.

Let us remember the words of Jesus himself on this crucial question: 'I am the resurrection and the life. He who believes in me will live, even though he dies; and whoever lives and believes in me will never die' (Jn. 11:25,26).

This is one of the most transcendental sentences Jesus ever pronounced. He becomes the guarantee for our own resurrection because he himself rose from the dead. Notice that the promise here, '[you] will live', means not just that you will survive, but that you will be resurrected; his statement '[you] will never die' does not mean a mere immortality of the soul, but the resurrection of the body (as we will see later on). This hope in a full and eternal life delivers the Christian from the natural horror of death and illuminates the darkness of dying and, subsequently, bereavement.

For this reason the Christian is able to sing with joy:

> Thine be the glory,
> Risen, conquering Son,
> Endless is the victory
> Thou o'er death hast won. ...

> Lo! Jesus meets us,
> Risen from the tomb!
> Lovingly He greets us,
> Scatters fear and gloom. ...

For her Lord now liveth,
Death hast lost its sting.

Christ has changed the meaning of death: dying as a transition

'I desire to depart and be with Christ, which is better by far' (Phil. 1:23). '... [for] the time has come for my departure' (2 Tim. 4:6).

If Christ has destroyed the power of death, then dying is just a transition to a fuller life. The Greek word translated 'to depart' was a nautical expression for releasing a vessel from its moorings. It also meant to strike the tent in order to move it to a different place. No doubt Paul was familiar with it as a tentmaker. For him dying was no more than a simple moving to a new 'address'. He used the same metaphor of the tent in 2 Corinthians 5:1: 'Now we know that if the earthly tent we live in is destroyed, we have a building from God, an eternal house in heaven, not built by human hands.' For this reason we proclaim with deep conviction that for Christians no good-bye is ever final.

Christ has changed the meaning of bereavement. How shall we then weep?

'... we do not want you to ... grieve like the rest of men, who have no hope' (1 Thes. 4:13).

What we have considered so far is indeed a source of comfort, but it does not remove the natural pain and distress of grief. Faith does not stop tears, but it changes their nature.

Remember again the several times that Jesus himself wept. He did so not only in front of Lazarus' corpse, but also, when he learned that John the Baptist had been executed, he felt the need to withdraw and grieve (Mt. 14:12,13). Even more outstanding is his own experience before death, in the Garden of Gethsemane, when he said to his most intimate friends: 'My

soul is overwhelmed with sorrow to the point of death. ...'
(Mt. 26:37,38). Very impressive also are words we read in
Hebrews: 'During the days of Jesus' life on earth, he offered
up prayers and petitions with loud cries and tears to the one
that could save him from death. ...' (Heb. 5:7).

The anxiety, the tears and the deep grief Jesus experienced
are the best answer to those Christians who claim that 'if you
had enough faith you would not cry.' There is no place in the
Bible for this kind of super-spirituality, that does not make us
more Christ-like, but less human. So grief is not only normal,
but healthy and necessary, even for Christians!

So we find ourselves somehow torn between two poles
here. From one side, death means separation and separation is
always hard, even when it is temporary. From the other side,
we firmly believe, on the basis of the facts we just considered,
that there is a precious new life after death. So there is tension
here, as in other areas of faith, between the present reality and
the future bliss. We need, therefore, a balance between the
tears that express deep pain and the confidence that is
inspired by our hope in Christ. We could summarise it by saying that 'Christians also weep, but their tears are full of hope.'
How is this expressed in practical terms? In other words, what
is the proper attitude of a Christian when touched by death?

Two examples will illustrate this principle of balance
between pain and faith.

Stephen, the first martyr of the early church has left us an
extraordinary challenge. We have chosen him as a model
because Stephen's martyrdom displayed in a magnificent way
three attitudes that every believer can show. Stephen faced
death

- *With peace.* 'All who were sitting in the Sanhedrin looked
  intently at Stephen, and they saw that his face was like the
  face of an angel' (Acts 6:15). He had just been slandered
  with serious false accusations (verses. 11, 12) that would
  lead inevitably to death. This plot to take his life was born
  out of intense envy from those who were supposed to be
  religious leaders: 'but they could not stand up against his

wisdom or the Spirit by which he spoke' (v.10). But in the midst of such an evil and ungodly crowd of people he shows an amazing quietness of spirit, to the point that all those around, who were his opponents, realised something unique in this godly deacon: 'his face was like the face of an angel.' How could a man under such circumstances have this deep peace? Faith is the answer.

- *With faith*. In times of grief, faith makes our eyes look up to heaven. 'But Stephen, full of the Holy Spirit, looked up to heaven and saw the glory of God, and Jesus standing at the right hand of God. "Look," he said, "I see heaven open and the Son of Man standing at the right hand of God"' (Acts 7:55,56). If Stephen had focused his attention on his slanderers and the terrible injustice he suffered, probably he would have reacted differently. But he had learned a lesson which is essential in times of deep distress and especially in times of bereavement: faith looks upwards, not downwards. Like Moses, faith made him endure as seeing 'him who is invisible' (Heb.11:27). One of the worst enemies in times of grief is self pity. Self-pity is the result of too much introspection. And introspection easily leads to desperation: 'poor me, how unfair all this is.' The bereaved should keep a balance between looking inwards – 'what is happening to me'– and looking upwards where the One who provides 'the hope which is an anchor for the soul, firm and secure' is sitting. Those who take hold of this hope, 'will be greatly encouraged' (see Heb. 6:18,19).
- *Without bitterness*. Stephen had many reasons to feel furious with those who were stoning him so unfairly and brutally. He could have died cursing his enemies or even bitterly blaming God for his 'passive silence' in the hour of death. This reaction would be perfectly reasonable before a crowd that was 'furious and gnashed their teeth at him' (7:54). But notice, instead, the very last words he pronounced before expiring: 'Then he fell on his knees and cried out, "Lord, do not hold this sin against them"' (v. 60). So impressive was the amazing attitude of this man 'full of the Holy Spirit' (v. 55), that the seeds for Paul's later conversion were planted

on this very tragedy: 'Meanwhile, the witnesses laid their clothes at the feet of a young man named Saul ... And Saul was there, giving approval to his death' (7:58 – 8:1). Stephen followed the steps of Christ who 'when they hurled their insults at him, he did not retaliate; when he suffered, he made no threats. Instead, he entrusted himself to him who judges justly' (1 Pet. 2:23).

The Scripture, nevertheless, is very realistic. Notice how the disciples reacted: after his death 'Godly men buried Stephen and mourned deeply for him' (Acts 8:2). Why did they weep if their beloved brother was with the Lord? Was not Stephen's glorious vision of heaven a confirmation of their faith? Was not the very resurrection of Jesus and his appearances still very recent? Why did they cry, then? Faith does not exclude pain. This reaction from the bereaved disciples is healthy. 'There is a time for everything, and a season for every activity under heaven' said the author of Ecclesiastes. In bereavement, there is a time for a robust expression of faith and peace; but likewise there is a time to mourn. One thing does not exclude the other. Mourning is not a sign of a poor faith; it is just a sign that the tough side of death – separation – deeply affects our delicate human emotions.

The second example is that of the apostle Paul. From his own experiences and his teaching about death we can also draw some more practical advice as to the Christian perspective on 'this last enemy'. Paul faced death

● *With joyful expectancy.* 'For me to live is Christ and to die is gain ...Yet what shall I choose? I do not know! I am torn between the two: I desire to depart and be with Christ, which is better by far' (Phil.1: 21-23). These words of Paul are a marvellous summary of his serene attitude before death. They exemplify a man who has conquered all fear of dying, although he lived under constant threats to his life. In fact, as he wrote these words, he was in prison in Rome, waiting for his martyrdom. As his own death was approaching, he shares his inner dilemma with the Philippian Christians: 'Yet what shall I choose? I do not know!' (v. 22b) I am in a strait, I am torn between the two desires...'

From one side, his pastoral responsibility made him wish to 'remain, and ... continue with all of you for your progress ...' (v. 25); on the other side, he felt a strong desire to 'depart' based on his confidence that dying means the entrance gate to the immediate presence of Christ. His expectation is so exciting that Paul uses a triple comparative to describe what death meant to him, literally 'much rather better', meaning 'by far the best': 'to be with Christ is by far the best'. No doubt this expectancy arose from his earnestness for a full intimacy with Christ, face to face. Paul knew one thing for sure: '... so we shall always be with the Lord' (1 Thes. 4:17, RSV). This is why he closes the text in 1 Thessalonians saying: 'Therefore encourage each other with these words' (1 Thes. 4:18).

- *With courage.* Courage is the opposite of fear. Paul wrote a great chapter on the resurrection of the dead and the new life in heaven, 1 Corinthians 15, which is a tremendous source of hope and encouragement to the bereaved. We shall consider part of it later on. Notice, nevertheless, how he closes this magnificent view of our future life with an exhortation that, apparently, comes as an anticlimax: 'Therefore, my dear brothers, stand firm. Let nothing move you' (v. 58).

It is somehow a surprising end. Why did Paul need to close his exposition with an appeal to steadfastness? Paul wanted his readers to take courage and not faint because this is the natural reaction, our human response when we face death. When Paul wrote his memorable statement, '[we] would prefer to be away from the body and at home with the Lord' (2 Cor. 5:8), he knew very well its two-fold implications. Being 'at home' with the Lord implies the departure of the 'earthly tent we live in' (v. 1) and such departure means a lot of tears and grief. He himself had experienced it in his very moving farewell to the elders in Ephesus (Acts 20:37,38, as we commented in chapter 2). In the same way, when he refers to Epaphroditus who 'was ill, and almost died' he adds: 'But God had mercy on him, and not on him only but also on me, to spare me sorrow upon sorrow' (Phil. 2:27).

Deep mourning, sorrow, tears and a lot of grief are the necessary expression of our pain when we leave this 'tent' even when we know that we are immediately going to our heavenly dwelling.

3 When dying is gain: our future in heaven

'For to me, to live is Christ and to die is gain ... We ... would prefer to be away from the body and at home with the Lord' (Phil. 1:21-23; 2 Cor. 5:8). How in the world can a person feel so confident before death? What was the secret of the apostle Paul which enabled him to speak about dying not only without fear, but even with optimism?

We already saw part of the answer a little earlier: death did not scare him because he understood that 'the last enemy' had been 'swallowed up in victory'. But there was something else in his spiritual experience which explains such hope and his earnestness to be with Christ: he came to know in a very clear way the wonders of the future life that were awaiting him after death. Central to his hope were the resurrection of the dead and the transformation into glorious bodies in the image of Christ: 'in a flash, in the twinkling of an eye, at the last trumpet. For the trumpet will sound, the dead will be raised imperishable, and we will be changed' (1 Cor. 15:52).

This magnificent glimpse of the future life nourished Paul's hope and moulded all his views on death. Now we will try to follow his steps and come to discover some basic facts which may enable us to face death and bereavement with a similar confidence.

What will heaven be like? We should be careful not to specu- late too much about the precise nature of heaven. Some have fallen into the temptation of guessing too many things and they ended with some fantastic record that, most likely, has little to do with reality. Many details about the future beyond death are hidden to us. The Bible, however, gives us a few guidelines which are clear enough to raise our expectancy and strengthen our hope. What has God told us in the Scriptures that heaven will be like?

Heaven as a relationship: to be with Christ

> Then I saw a new heaven and a new earth, for the first heaven and the first earth had passed away ... And I heard a loud voice from the throne saying, 'Now the dwelling of God is with men, and he will live with them. They will be his people and God himself will be with them and be their God' (Rev. 21:1,3).

Heaven is primarily to be with Christ and to be like Christ. This is the core of the teaching of Scripture. It is indeed a place: '... I saw a new heaven and a new earth' are the opening words of this triumphant text of Revelation 21. But it is above all a relationship, the perfect relationship, face to face, without any interference, with the Father and with Christ. For 'Now we see but a poor reflection ... then we shall see [him] face to face' (1 Cor.13:12a). It was this certainty of being 'present with Christ' that made Paul desire with all his heart to finish his life here on earth and 'to be clothed with our heavenly dwelling' (2 Cor. 5:2).

The story of the Transfiguration also gives us a glimpse of how pleasant and desirable this condition must be. '[Jesus] was transfigured before them. His face shone like the sun, and his clothes became as white as the light' (Mt. 17:2). The three privileged apostles, Peter, John and James, were enjoying the presence of Christ in this glorious environment so much that Peter proposed to remain there: 'Lord, it is good for us to be here. If you wish, I will put three shelters – one for you, one for Moses and one for Elijah' (v. 4). They were overwhelmed by the beauty and majesty of the transfigured Christ.

Therefore, the centre of life in heaven is not the 'ego', but the 'us': a precious two-fold relationship, with Christ and with all the saints. Of course, there will be many glorious blessings to be enjoyed in heaven (see the description of the new Jerusalem in Revelation 21:9-27). Nevertheless these wonders of Paradise that Paul described as 'inexpressible things' (2 Cor. 12:4) are the consequence of being there, not its purpose. The emphasis of life in heaven is not hedonistic – on enjoying ourselves; but relational – to be with. In this sense, the Christian idea of heaven differs a lot from other religions where the emphasis lies on a selfish enjoyment of many pleasures, specially the ones that were forbidden on earth. This radical difference is one more example of the fact that not all religions are the same thing. Opposite to this reality, hell is the eternal separation from God, that place where God is absent. The absence of God is the hallmark of life in hell.

Heaven as a perfect state: to be like Christ

> Dear friends, now we are children of God, and what we will be has not yet been made known. But we know that when he appears, we shall be like him, for we shall see him as he is (1 Jn. 3:2).

If the first great privilege of heaven is to be face to face with Christ, the second most magnificent gift is that we will become like Christ. The ultimate goal of our Christian life is to become like Jesus, to be transformed into his likeness because he is our perfect model.

This perfection will be fully accomplished in heaven because 'just as we have borne the likeness of the earthly man, so shall we bear the likeness of the man from heaven' (1 Cor. 15:49). How this will be performed remains a mystery, but it is, nevertheless, a firm promise according to Paul

> Listen, I tell you a mystery: We will not all sleep [die], but we will all be changed, in a flash, in the twinkling of an eye, at the last trumpet ... The dead will be raised imperishable, and we will be changed. For the perishable must clothe itself with the

imperishable, and the mortal with immortality ... then the saying that is written will come true: 'Death has been swallowed up in victory' (1 Cor. 15: 51-54).

We are eager to know in what practical ways we are going to be like Christ. We cannot speculate on the precise details, but some features are quite clear according to the Scripture.

- *There will be a resurrection of the body, not a mere immortality.* The Christian hope is not the survival of the soul, but the resurrection of the body. We are promised a new body, not just a shadowy immortality of our spirit. Most religions envisage some form of survival, either in an impersonal collective existence or in individual reincarnation as in Buddhism. Actually this hope in some diffused kind of immortality is essential to any religion. Christianity, however, departs utterly from this view of eternity. We will have transformed bodies in the same way that the risen Christ had a transformed body of glory.
- *Our personal identity will be preserved.* The resurrection of the believer will preserve our individuality in such a way that the essence of our identity will be kept in heaven. One of the most precious attributes that God gave us is our uniqueness: each human being is a unique creature, without a possibility of being copied. This personal and distinctive identity will continue in heaven. This means that, as a principle, I will continue to be myself.
- *We will have a body of glory.* Our resurrected bodies will, therefore, retain some kind of resemblance to our present bodies. Jesus, after the resurrection, still had the nail marks in his hands and the scars of the crucifixion. He told the doubting Thomas: 'Put your finger here; see my hands. Reach out your hand and put it into my side. Stop doubting and believe' (Jn. 20:27).

Whereas it is true that the disciples sometimes had difficulties in recognising him e.g. the two disciples of Emmaus – it is striking to notice how quickly Mary of Magdala recognised

Jesus by his voice, in spite of her initial difficulties: '... she turned round and saw Jesus standing there, but she did not realise that it was Jesus. ... [He] said to her, "Mary." She turned towards him and cried "Rabboni!" ...' (Jn. 20:14-16). Jesus' voice kept its uniqueness and this allowed Mary to identify him instantly. In fact we know today that our voice is like our fingerprints: there are no two human beings with the same voice; it is something unique for each person.

In the same way as the disciples could recognise the risen Christ, so we have many reasons to believe that we will be able to recognise one another in heaven. Let us remember the Transfiguration experience when the three apostles could perfectly identify Moses and Elijah and have some kind of relationship with them. This hope is one of the uplifting promises which greatly relieve the pain of separation. The possibility of seeing and being again with the loved ones is certainly a powerful balm for the bereaved.

Our bodies, however, will also be transformed – our life there will be new and different. Free from sickness and the effects of age, it will be a body of glory, reflecting the glory of God, a body full of beauty and splendour. Also it will be a body with special powers, ready to fulfil its new purposes in heaven.

Heaven as a place: our eternal house in heaven

> Now we know that if the earthly tent we live in is destroyed, we have a building from God, an eternal house in heaven, not built by human hands. Meanwhile we groan, longing to be clothed with our heavenly dwelling (2 Cor. 5:1,2).

Paul compares our current life to a tent. The hallmark of a tent is its fragility; it can be damaged easily. In fact, he reminded his readers a bit earlier that 'outwardly [that is our body, our health] we are wasting away' (4:16). There is an inevitable process of decay in our 'tent' which eventually leads to its destruction. Indeed our life on this earth is very fragile and we may be called to leave the tent unexpectedly at any moment.

If we consider our human existence only from this side – life is short and fragile – there are not many reasons for optimism. But 'Now'– here Paul introduces one of his striking contrasts – when this earthly dwelling is destroyed, we have another house which is far better. And then he deliberately compares both dwellings and describes to us the features of our new address.

- It is a building, not a tent: a much more solid structure.
- The builder and architect is God himself: it is not made by human hands.
- It is located in heaven, not on this earth.

The whole picture is, thus, clear in Paul's eyes: there is a solid, eternal, imperishable building prepared for the believers in Christ. For this reason Paul prefers to 'at home with the Lord' (v. 8). It is indeed better to live in such a house than in a tent! How encouraging it is to remember that Jesus himself promised us this future dwelling in heaven: 'In my Father's house are many rooms; if it were not so, I would have told you. I am going there to prepare a place for you. And if I go and prepare a place for you, I will come back and take you to be with me that you also may be where I am' (Jn. 14:1-3).

It is difficult to read these words without being moved! Notice the context of tribulation in which they were pronounced: Jesus' death was very near. Our Lord had one purpose clearly in mind: to comfort his disciples and prepare them for the sad events which were about to come. Jesus anticipates their bereavement and strengthens their hope with the wonderful promise of the heavenly 'rooms' in the house of the Father. Therefore, says Jesus, 'Do not let your hearts be troubled. Trust in God; trust also in me' (v.1). This is our logical reaction when we contemplate this new house reserved and prepared for us, because we have 'an inheritance that can never perish, spoil or fade – kept in heaven for you' (1 Pet. 1:4).

Heaven as a great reunion: the wedding supper of the Lamb

> After this I looked and there before me was a great multitude that
> no-one could count, from every nation, tribe, people and language,
> standing before the throne and in front of the Lamb (Rev. 7:9).

As we pointed out earlier, the essence of heaven lies in its relationships: to God and Christ first, but also to all our brothers
and sisters who make the great family of Christ. Thus, our life
in heaven will not be an individual experience. The body
dimension it envisages is one of the most precious elements in
our hope. Heaven is described in the New Testament, especially in Revelation, as the great gathering of all the saints, all
those who believed in Jesus Christ. The great reunion will be
so joyful and glorious that it is compared to a wedding supper.
It is indeed the wedding banquet of the Lamb: 'Then the angel
said to me: "Write: Blessed are those who are invited to the
wedding supper of the Lamb!" ...' (Rev. 19:9).

What is the conclusion, then, of such a magnificent reality?

No more tears, no more death, no more mourning

> '[God] will wipe every tear from their eyes. There will be no
> more death or mourning or crying or pain, for the old order of
> things has passed away.' He who was seated on the throne
> said: 'I am making everything new!' (Rev. 21:4,5).

So far we described heaven in positive terms: what it will be
like. But we are also told very clearly what things will not exist
in heaven any more; the text in Revelation defines heaven also
in negative terms. John, following God's revelation, states
clearly that the most painful realities of this present life will
disappear. He mentions five examples, but the list could be
longer. The ones he includes are particularly relevant to the
bereaved: no more tears, death, mourning, crying or pain.

All these terrible realities will disappear because Christ
'makes everything new' in the new heaven and earth. All
forms of suffering will be changed into joy, the great joy of a

life where there is no evil whatsoever, the joy of a dwelling where the very presence of Christ illuminates all shadow (see Rev. 21:23,24). Even many years before Christ was born, God anticipated this joy through the prophet Isaiah: 'Behold, I will create new heavens and a new earth. The former things will not be remembered, nor will they come to mind. But be glad and rejoice for ever in what I will create' (Is. 65:17,18).

Be glad and rejoice because there is hope for the future. The only condition for participating in such a glorious reunion is to drink from the water of life that Christ offers to each human being: 'I am the Alpha and the Omega, the Beginning and the End. To him who is thirsty I will give to drink without cost from the spring of the water of life.' (Rev. 21:6)

As this magnificent perspective is disclosed before us, our attitude towards death changes. It is true that we cannot change our circumstances – a loss cannot be repaired – but it is also true that we can look at these same circumstances with different eyes. It is the eyes of faith that allow us to contemplate the rising of the rainbow after the storm. The violent storm of death is followed by the quietness of the rainbow. The rainbow symbolises the covenant God made with the human race: in Christ, life wins over death. Therefore: 'Do not be afraid. I am the First and the Last. I am the Living One; I was dead, and behold I am alive for ever and ever! And I hold the keys of death …' (Rev. 1:17,18)

* * *

John and Ali Risbridger have lost two baby boys: Daniel died at thirteen days old in 1993 and then, three years later, they had a stillborn son, Jonathan.

John Risbridger

How did you come to terms with the two deaths, as a Christian?

I think talking to other people means you have to think it through, but also the sense of God's presence in the experience with Daniel was so strong. If you have any integrity at all, you have to do some integrating at some point... you can't just have one box that has an experience of God that is very real and another box in your brain that's just completely dominated by a 'Why?' question that has no answers. I think I'd have fallen apart if I had stayed in that position for too long. The summer before we lost Daniel, I read a book by Don Carson, called *How long, O Lord?* which was on suffering ... and it was immensely helpful. I read it again the summer afterwards, to say to myself, 'I've seen this now from the inside rather than the outside, does it still work?' and it did still work. It was still very helpful.

Did you grieve differently each time?

With Jonathan it was a totally different thing. For the first 24, 36 hours we didn't engage with having lost Jonathan at all, which is probably not that healthy, though it is inevitable. It means that right from the start, you're beginning to freeze out certain emotions. Emotions are very complex anyway in the case of a stillbirth. We both found that we cried a lot less with Jonathan. With Daniel we were crying half the time really, and readily crying with each other, but Alison cried very little with Jonathan. I didn't cry that much. We found it harder to communicate with each other, because there hadn't been all the normal things of a relationship [with the baby]. All there was [was] this cold reality of a baby that wasn't there, except his body. We spent quite a lot of time with Jonathan's body in the room with us, and we handled him, showed him to our parents, and we still have a picture of him on our wall in our bedroom, as we do of Daniel, but it felt like the least bad form of coping with it, rather than a good form.

It was worse because you hadn't known Jonathan?

Absolutely. It was my first experience of being a father with Daniel and I had no idea how strong the paternal emotions are. If I'd needed to mortgage my house, give up my job, I'd have done anything in the world to save his life. Sometimes the medical staff didn't understand how your need to feel like a parent is very strong when you have a baby in the Special Care Baby Unit. There are very few things that you can do that reinforce that bond, because you can't hold the baby, but there are some things, they call them 'cares', which means changing the baby's nappy, giving them a little wash, and those things suddenly assume this enormous significance because they're the only expression of being a parent that you have, other than just being there. It's extraordinary how strong a parent-child bond forms around little things like that. And the grief, when it came, was clean grief; we knew where to locate it. There was a relationship that had begun which was now broken, and so we knew why we were feeling as we did.

With Jonathan there wasn't any of that. There was just that we didn't have a baby. We tried to bond by holding his body, but he'd come straight out of a body fridge, he was cold. It's just very hard. I think that is why it was a much more complex experience, psychologically and spiritually. We were both a bit more withdrawn.

Was there a feeling that you had been here once and didn't want to go back?

I don't think there was, to be honest. I think we would almost have done anything to feel like we felt before, because we really emerged from the experience with Daniel feeling that it was a terrible experience but also an incredible experience. God was very gracious and put a lot of things around us to help us make it as good as it could be, and we knew then that God could be close to you in the middle of pain. With Jonathan, most of those things weren't there to anything like the same extent. The issue wasn't 'Can we expect God to put us in a cotton wool nest and make us feel OK?' It was much more of a gut issue: 'Will we keep trusting even though it hurts much more and feels much more confusing and complex?' It didn't feel like there were lots of things that we were going to learn by going through it twice that we couldn't have learnt by just going through it once. It was a much more brutal test of faith. Will we still come out of this saying 'God is good'? Will we still be saying 'Though the fig tree doesn't blossom and there's no fruit on the vine, yet I will rejoice in the Lord'? We had to look around us and say, 'Would it be right to judge God's goodness simply on the basis of what has happened to us now?' Look at the rest of our lives: we've got families that love us, we've got a church family that means lots to us, we've got the hope of eternal life for us and our children, we know God, now we've got two wonderful kids – lots of riches in life. Is it really right to come to an evaluation of God's goodness on the basis of one experience?

People often find that the problem of suffering is the main reason why they can't believe in God. My human reaction to suffering ends up making me, forcing me, to adopt a worldview with God in the picture. Because anyone who claims to react to suffering without there being a moral dimension to their reaction is denying their humanness. We all respond to things in moral categories. We say 'this shouldn't be' but it is senseless to say that something shouldn't be a certain way unless you have some basis for saying what it should be. Give that basis whatever label you may choose for the sake of argument, but it's God in some form or other. The experience of suffering, and the way that I inevitably attach moral categories to that experience, actually drives me back to Theism.

In suffering you get this co-existence; the miracle of life, this extraordinary thing called humanity; we find ourselves relating to this baby, even though there is hardly any basis for a relationship with it, we are bonded to this thing as a human being in a very profound sense and the wonder of creation hits you ... but at the same time the brokenness of creation hits you as well. Suffering very often has those two next to each other. The only reason that we feel so strongly that this shouldn't be is because we feel intuitively that creation is good, that there is something wonderful there. That creation/fall story, as a basis for understanding the world, and understanding suffering, for me having gone through it, is still a far more plausible way of looking at the world than someone who reduces suffering to just cold cause and effect.

So many biblical themes become relevant after experiences such as these ... the Incarnation, the Man of Sorrows, acquainted with grief. Psalm 34 says God is 'close to the broken-hearted and saves those who are crushed in spirit.' We watched our son die, God watched his Son die, and yet he did it for us. He chose to do it. The resonances are so strong. It seems to me ultimately that it is only the cross that brings together suffering and God, who enters human suffering in order to redeem humanity.

The 'Why?' question does bite. There is no doubt about that. Whatever solution you end up with, unless you are going to deny the humanity, you have to accept there's an element of mystery in it.

For further information

The *Bereaved Parents Network* was set up by Peter and Barbie Reynolds, whose stories are part of this book. They can be contacted via Care for the Family. Tel: 029 2081 0800 fax: 029 2081 4089: email mail@cff.org.uk

Cruse Bereavement Care have a phone helpline 0870 167 1677 and an email helpline: helpline@crusebereavementcare.org.uk and also a freephone number for young people aged twelve to eighteen: 0808 808 1677.

The Compassionate Friends (TCF) is an organisation for bereaved parents and their families offering understanding, support and encouragement to others after the death of a child or children. They also offer support, advice and information to other relatives, friends and professionals who are helping the family. Email: info@tcf.org.uk Helpline: 0117 953 9639. This helpline is always answered by a bereaved parent who is there to listen and they can also put people in touch with their nearest local contact and provide information about TCF's services. The helpline is open every day of the year: 10 am – 4 pm and 6.30 pm – 10.30 pm GMT.

Bereaved children: the *Childhood Bereavement Network* (part of the National Children's Bureau) lists information on all the local children's bereavement support services. The services their directory covers can be contacted for information, guidance and support by anyone who is caring for a child who has been bereaved, or by the child themselves. To contact them, telephone 020 7843 6309. Fax: 020 7843 1439. Email: cbn@ncb.org.uk

Winston's Wish works with bereaved children and is based in Gloucestershire. Tel: 01242 515157. Email: info@ winstonswish.org.uk

Richmond's Hope works with bereaved children in Scotland and is based in Edinburgh. Tel: 0131 661 6818. Email Richmondshope@tiscali.co.uk